Censorship

Recent Titles in
Historical Guides to Controversial Issues in America

Censorship

Mark Paxton

Historical Guides to Controversial Issues in America

GREENWOOD PRESS
Westport, Connecticut • London

Library of Congress Cataloging-in-Publication Data

Paxton, Mark, 1957–
  Censorship / Mark Paxton.
      p. cm. — (Historical guides to controversial issues in America, ISSN 1541–0021)
  Includes bibliographical references and index.
  ISBN 978–0–313–33751–2 (alk. paper)
  1. Censorship—United States—History.   I. Title.
  Z658.U5P39   2008
  363.310973—dc22   2008011156

British Library Cataloging in Publication Data is available.

Copyright © 2008 by Mark Paxton

Library of Congress Catalog Card Number: 2008011156
ISBN: 978–0–313–33751–2
ISSN: 1541–0021

First published in 2008

Greenwood Press, 88 Post Road West, Westport, CT 06881
An imprint of Greenwood Publishing Group, Inc.
www.greenwood.com

Printed in the United States of America

The paper used in this book complies with the
Permanent Paper Standard issued by the National
Information Standards Organization (Z39.48–1984).

10 9 8 7 6 5 4 3 2 1

Contents

Preface

Attempting to write a book about the history of censorship in America is somewhat akin to attempting to write a book about the history of the nation; it is a daunting task to squeeze in everything important, omitting the minor or inconsequential while leaving out nothing of importance. Scholars have written volumes on each area of censorship, and a book such as this can do little more than highlight the significant and try to put it into context.

Being an author, although at times a solitary endeavor, requires copious amounts of help from others. First, I would like to thank my wife, Margaret Weaver, and our son, Jesse Weaver Paxton, for putting up with my seizure of one end of the dining room table for my assorted research material and laptop computer, for enduring my seemingly endless writing, and for not complaining when I obsessed over various chapters and frantically tried to meet deadlines. A tremendous thank you also goes to Margaret for spending hour after hour after hour poring over my manuscript and making uncountable suggestions for improvements (although any errors that did creep into the manuscript are solely my fault).

I would also like to thank Missouri State University, the College of Arts and Letters, and the Department of Media, Journalism, and Film for granting me a one-semester sabbatical so that I could get started on the book once I signed the contract with Greenwood. My students at Missouri State also deserve thanks for putting up with my schedule, in which I devoted most Tuesdays and Thursdays during several semesters to work on this book. The staff at Meyer Library on the Missouri State University campus also aided tremendously in helping me track down innumerable books that were available only on other campuses.

I would also be remiss if I did not thank my editors at Greenwood. Steven Vetrano was my first editor and contacted me about writing this book, which I probably would never have considered on my own. He was replaced as my editor by Sarah Colwell and then Sandy Towers. I'd also like to thank the copy editor, Kimberly Miller, as well as Mary Cotofan and the staff at Apex CoVantage, who did the hands-on work with the manuscript.

Introduction

A. J. Brown, a young woman in Durham, North Carolina, got a visit from Federal Bureau of Investigation (FBI) agents in 2003 and was questioned for 40 minutes about "un-American" materials in her apartment. The FBI started a formal file on her. What was the offense that brought her under federal investigation? She had a poster on her wall criticizing the 152 executions that occurred in Texas when President George W. Bush was governor.[1] Brown ran afoul of the USA PATRIOT Act, enacted in the wake of the September 11, 2001, terrorist attacks. She was not alone.

Andrew O'Connell, a public defender who was using a public computer at the Santa Fe, New Mexico, library, became involved in a debate with another library patron and was overheard stating that "Bush is out of control." He found himself surrounded by four police officers, and Secret Service agents handcuffed and detained him while they questioned him about his political statements.[2]

Many people believe that censorship is a relic of the past, that there is no need for a book about censorship in this modern era of freedom of speech and the press. Many of those same people might be shocked to learn that although censorship was common during and after the founding of this country, it also continues today. The First Amendment of the Constitution, in 43 words, lists some of the fundamental rights that American citizens enjoy: "Congress shall make no law respecting an establishment of religion or prohibiting the free exercise thereof; abridging freedom of speech or of the press; or the right of the people peaceably to assemble, and to petition the Government for a redress of grievances." Even that guarantee, however, is not absolute. The U.S. Supreme Court, for instance, has ruled that entire categories of expression—such as obscenity, libel, and "fighting words"[3]—are subject to less protection than other types of speech and press. The broadcast media are regulated by the Federal Communications Commission (FCC), which imposes its own rules that, for example, require broadcast stations to air political commercials in the weeks preceding an election,[4] limit the number and content of commercials during mandatory children's programming on television, and prohibit programming that is indecent but not obscene—that is, offensive but not designed to arouse the viewer sexually.[5] In addition, the news media face restrictions when reporting from the scene of military conflicts. High school students and, increasingly, their counterparts on college campuses face limits on what they can write in student publications.[6] Motion pictures are subject to a ratings system, and television programs carry symbols (such as TV-M for shows suitable for adult audiences only or TV-Y for shows suitable for all audiences). Access to the Internet is subject to control in schools and public libraries, which are required by the federal government to use filters to limit access to inappropriate sites.

These attempts to restrict access to material are not a twenty-first- or even twentieth-century development. The Alien and Sedition Act of 1798, enacted by Congress just seven years after the First Amendment was ratified, made it a crime punishable by fine and imprisonment to write or speak anything "false, malicious or scandalous" against the government, Congress, or the president with the intent to bring them into contempt or disrepute or to excite the hatred of the people—in other words, it was a crime to criticize the president or other members of the ruling Federalist Party. Hundreds went to jail for violating this act, including U.S. Representative Matthew Lyon.[7] Anthony Comstock championed laws banning "lewd" material from the mail in 1873; then, after Congress passed the Comstock Act, the post office appointed him chief censor of the mails. African American slaves and even freed former slaves after the Civil War did not have the right to free speech in the 1800s.[8] Neither did women until the suffrage movement.

It might appear a simple matter to discount some of these efforts to limit expression as absurd or even outrageous. At the same time, however, each of these limits is rooted in the belief that one of the central roles of our government is to protect citizens from harmful material. The question for legal scholars, political figures, and others has always been: How far do we go in protecting people from what is perceived to be harmful? Sociologist W. Phillips Davison, in a 1983 journal article, postulates a fascinating hypothesis called the third-person effect that could help to explain why some people seek to limit or censor the information made available to others, including pornography, hate speech, television programming, movies, or politically sensitive media messages.[9]

Davison's third-person effect hypothesis consists of two main concepts. First, people tend to overestimate the effect that persuasive communication has on others. Second, any effect that the communication achieves may be attributable not to the individual message recipient but also to that individual's belief that the communication is having an effect on others. According to Davison,

In its broadest formulation, this hypothesis predicts that people will tend to overestimate the influence that mass communications have on the attitudes and behaviors of others. More specifically, individuals who are members of an audience that is exposed to persuasive communication (whether or not this communication is intended to be persuasive) will expect the communication to have a greater impact on others than on themselves. And whether or not these individuals are among the *ostensible* audience for the message, the impact that they expect this communication to have on others may lead them to take some action. Any effect that the communication achieves may thus be due not to the reaction of the ostensible audience but rather to the behavior of those who anticipate, or think they perceive, some reaction on the part of others.[10]

To summarize his hypothesis, Davison states, "In the view of those trying to evaluate the effects of communication, its greatest impact will be not on 'me' or 'you,' but on 'them'—the third persons."[11]

Since Davison's theory was published, a number of researchers have found that the third-person effect could explain many instances of censorship; people report in surveys and demonstrate during experiments that they do not believe themselves to be affected by harmful material such as pornography or violent television programming, but do believe that others—the third persons—are affected and must be protected. Whether this protection is warranted has occupied scholars and the nation's greatest legal minds since the 1700s.

Any discussion of censorship in America, however, must begin with a look at freedom of expression and limits on that expression before this nation was founded, because many of our laws came to us from Europe, particularly from England.[12] Chapter 1 examines the history of censorship of dissent, focusing on the concepts of freedom of expression and limits on that expression as they developed along with the passage of the Constitution and the Bill of Rights. Chapter 2 examines government control of the news media during wartime, ranging from the Civil War to the War in Iraq, and the often contentious relationship between the news media and the military.

Chapter 3 focuses on control of what we read in books, one of the most contentious areas of the debate over free expression versus censorship. This chapter also discusses the controversy over what books are made available in public schools, a dispute that erupted into violence in one West Virginia community in 1974, including the dynamiting of the school board office and the firebombing of schools.

Chapter 4 examines the long history of government attempts to regulate the visual arts, particularly motion pictures, plays, music, and television as well as painting, photography, and the other fine arts. This chapter includes a discussion of the Hays Code, the Roman Catholic Church's Legion of Decency, and innumerable local review boards, which determined what was acceptable in motion pictures, as well as the role that television networks played in censoring their own programming. It also looks at plays and other dramatic works that have been banned by local governments and concludes with a discussion of the attempted censorship in Cincinnati in 1990 of Robert Mapplethorpe's homoerotic photography.

Chapter 5 considers the limits on sexually explicit material and the long history of government attempts to define what is obscene versus what is acceptable for consumption. In particular, this chapter examines the Supreme Court's 1973 decision in *Miller v. California,* which used a three-part test to determine whether material is obscene, as well as more recent attempts to limit access to material that does not meet the *Miller* standard for obscenity.

Chapter 6 provides an examination of the First Amendment rights students have and court decisions that grant or limit those rights, including the 1969 Supreme Court decision stating that public school students have the right to free speech that does not materially disrupt the classroom[13] and extending to more recent decisions rescinding those student First Amendment rights. The conclusion, chapter 7, examines where censorship might be headed as we enter the twenty-first century, in an era of exploding access to information through the Internet, satellite television, cell phones that also serve as e-mail systems, and online video viewing.

As a final comment, writing a book about censorship is a daunting task. New instances of censorship and court decisions either upholding or overturning that censorship are continually taking place. Almost by definition, a book about censorship is out of date nearly before the ink is dry on the page. For that reason, this book focuses on the history of censorship in America, taking a broad look at where this country has been and where it might be heading. In addition, although it might seem simple to state opposition to censorship in favor of the right to free expression, in reality it is much more challenging. Where does an American citizen's constitutional right to freedom under the First Amendment conflict with the government's goal of protecting us? This is a question on which reasonable people can differ, and it is the central issue of this book.

NOTES

1. Susan Gladin, "Watching Out for Civil Liberties," *Chapel Hill Herald,* September 14, 2003, 2.

2. Sam Stanton and Emily Bazar, "Agents Abridge Rights," *The (Raleigh) News and Observer*, September 28, 2003.

3. Both obscenity and fighting words will be discussed in later chapters. Libel, the written defamation of a person with false material, is a large and complex area of media law that deserves a book of its own. On libel, see Russell L. Weaver, Andrew T. Kenyon, David F. Partlett, and Clive P. Walker, *The Right to Speak Ill: Defamation, Reputation and Free Speech* (Durham, NC: Carolina Academic Press, 2006); Paul Siegel, *Cases in Communication Law* (Boston: Allyn and Bacon, 2002), 46–89; and Anthony Lewis, *Make No Law: The Sullivan Case and the First Amendment* (New York: Vintage Books, 1993).

4. Section 315 of the Federal Communications Act requires all over-the-air stations, if they sell or give time to a candidate for political office 45 days before a primary election or 60 days before a general election, to provide the same opportunity to all other candidates for the same office. A similar provision, Section 312 (a) 7, requires stations to provide access (free or paid) during the same time frame to candidates for federal office (president, vice president, U.S. senators, and U.S. representatives).

5. *FCC v. Pacifica*, 438 U.S. 726 (1978). The Supreme Court upheld the FCC's ruling punishing a radio station for airing a George Carlin comedy routine about the seven words you cannot say on the air. The distinction between indecency and obscenity is discussed later in this book.

6. In 1988, the Supreme Court, in *Hazelwood v. Kuhlmeier,* ruled that administrators in public secondary schools have wide latitude in controlling the content of student expression that is part of the curriculum, such as a school newspaper. In 2006, the Supreme Court declined to consider an appeal of a case in Illinois, *Hosty v. Carter,* that applied the same standard to student publications at public colleges and universities, leaving open the question whether *Hazelwood* applies to colleges.

7. Aleine Austin, *Matthew Lyon: "New Man" of the Democratic Revolution, 1749–1822* (University Park: Pennsylvania State University Press, 1981), 105. This law was so unpopular that Lyon was re-elected to Congress while serving his sentence.

8. Clement Eaton, *The Freedom-of-Thought Struggle in the Old South* (New York: Harper Torchbooks, 1964).

9. W. Phillips Davison, "The Third-Person Effect in Communication," *Public Opinion Quarterly* 47 (1983): 1–15.

10. Ibid., 3.

11. Ibid.

12. Both our common law and many aspects of our legal system were developed in colonial days based on those in effect in England. A discussion of this is available in any book that touches on the history of American law, such as Douglas M. Fraleigh and Joseph S. Tuman's book, *Freedom of Speech in the Marketplace of Ideas* (New York: St. Martin's Press, 1997), 46–66.

13. *Tinker v. Des Moines Independent School District,* 393 U.S. 503 (1969).

1

Censorship of Dissent

John Frohnmayer, the former chairman of the National Endowment for the Arts who later became a First Amendment scholar, contends, "Ironically, in spite of the First Amendment, America has a robust history of repression, intolerance and censorship."[1] It is difficult to argue with him, particularly in the area of dissent against government policies or officials.

The birth of the Constitution was not easy. Most of the laws that were in effect in the colonies before the Revolutionary War came to this country from England, where repression of individual rights was common. Among these common-law imports was the notion of seditious libel, which made it a crime to speak or write anything that criticized the government, whether true or not. Punishments could be severe. In 1663 England, the printer John Twyn was judged to have printed a book that endorsed the right to revolution. He was found guilty of treason and sentenced to be hanged by the neck, cut down while still alive, emasculated, disemboweled, quartered, and beheaded. The message was clear: do not criticize the government.

In this country, the notion of seditious libel was not supported by much of the public. One the most publicized tests of the notion of seditious libel occurred in 1735 in the trial of John Peter Zenger, the publisher of the *New York Weekly Journal,* who had published inflammatory articles criticizing the colonial governor of New York, William Cosby. Zenger was charged with seditious libel. The judge ruled during the trial that if Zenger had published the offending publication, and Zenger admitted that he had, then the jury had no recourse other than to find him guilty. Zenger's lawyer, Andrew Hamilton, argued in a lengthy and persuasive statement to the jury, however, that Zenger had the right to criticize the government: "It is not the case of one poor printer, nor of New York alone, which you are now trying. No! Its consequence affects every free man that lives under British government on the main of America. It is the cause of liberty."[2] The jury ultimately agreed with Hamilton's argument that truth was a defense against seditious libel, freeing Zenger.[3]

Other printers and newspaper publishers ran afoul of seditious libel laws, perhaps most notably Benjamin Franklin's brother James, who was briefly imprisoned for suggesting in his *New England Courant* that the Massachusetts colonial government was less than enthusiastic about pursuing a band of pirates.[4] In another situation, a New York Assembly member threatened to torture an unwilling witness who refused to testify about whether he had published a handbill criticizing that same assembly,[5] and scores of people were brought before colonial assemblies because of their speech or publications. One of the reasons those in the colonies fought for their independence was to win freedom from government repression. But when the founding fathers met in Philadelphia to chart the course for the new nation, they could not agree on what individual rights would be included in the new Constitution. Some argued that the document should establish only the framework of the federal government, whereas others, most notably Thomas Jefferson and George Mason, argued that the Constitution should also protect individual rights. A compromise was reached. The Constitution would be sent to the states for ratification without the provision of individual rights, followed by a separate set of amendments guaranteeing individual rights that would receive a separate ratification vote.

THE SEDITION ACT OF 1798

The First Amendment, guaranteeing freedom of speech, the press, religion, assembly, and petition of government, was adopted as part of that Bill of Rights in 1791, just two years after ratification of the Constitution.[6] Even though the First Amendment prohibited Congress from abridging freedom of speech or the press, it took only seven years for Congress to do just that.

The two major political parties in America were the Federalists and the Republicans (not to be confused with today's Republican Party). The Federalists were in power in 1798, with John Adams in the presidency and the party controlling both the U.S. Senate and the U.S. House of Representatives. The Federalists believed that war with France, with whom the United States had been engaged in a sometimes difficult treaty, was inevitable. Ostensibly, the Sedition Act of 1798 was aimed at calming criticism over the federal government's negotiations with the French; in reality, though, it targeted the Federalists' political opponents, the Republicans.[7]

The Sedition Act stated that

if any person shall write, print, utter or publish scandalous and malicious writing or writings against the government of the United States, or either House of the Congress of the United States, or the President of the United States, with intent to defame... or to bring them...into contempt or disrepute; or to excite against them...the hatred of the good people of the United States, or to stir up sedition within the United States...then such person...shall be punished by a fine not exceeding two thousand dollars, and by imprisonment not exceeding two years.[8]

This new law was used as a weapon by the Federalists against Republicans and their sympathizers. Among those convicted of violating the Sedition Act was U.S. Congressman Matthew Lyon of Vermont, who was found guilty of criticizing President Adams and sentenced to four months in jail, where he served his time in a dungeon with horse thieves and other felons; as a sign of the unpopularity of this law, Lyon was re-elected to Congress while serving his sentence.[9] Also sentenced to prison was Thomas Cooper, who was charged with writing an anonymous article in the *Reading (Pennsylvania) Weekly Advertiser* criticizing President Adams. In his defense, he argued that Adams was not "blessed with political infallibility," but he was convicted anyway.[10]

Those targeted by the law included Republicans Thomas Jefferson and James Madison, who wrote a resolution, adopted by the state legislatures of Kentucky and Virginia, opposing the Sedition Act; because they feared arrest for their actions, they kept their role secret. Opposition to the Sedition Act grew, with the number of Republican partisan newspapers increasing from fewer than 20 to more than 50 in two years. In 1802, Jefferson was narrowly elected president, with Lyon, ironically, casting the tie-breaking vote in the House of Representatives. (Jefferson was in an electoral college tie with Aaron Burr, which threw the election to the House of Representatives.)[11] Once in office, Jefferson issued pardons of everyone who had been convicted of violating the Sedition Act, which had been allowed to expire, and Congress, now controlled by Republicans, voted to repay the fines of those convicted.[12]

Jefferson, although viewed by many as a founding father of the First Amendment, was not always enamored with the free press. Complaining about negative press coverage of his administration, Jefferson argued that although the First Amendment prevented federal censorship, the states were free to impose restrictions.[13] That legal philosophy prevailed until the U.S. Supreme Court ruled in the 1925 *Gitlow v. New York* case that the First Amendment applies to all forms of government through the due process clause of the 14th Amendment, which guaranteed, in part: "No state shall make or enforce any law which shall abridge the privileges or immunities of citizens of the United States; nor shall any state deprive any person of life, liberty, or property, without due process of law; nor deny to any person within its jurisdiction the equal protection of the laws...."[14]

THE SOUTH, THE CIVIL WAR, AND RECONSTRUCTION

In the years before the 1925 *Gitlow* decision, state censorship of speech and press was quite common. An 1824 decision in a New York court, in *Root v. King,* made it easier for government officials to sue publications for libel, leading to a huge increase in libel suits in that state.[15] In the South in the years leading up to the Civil War, most state legislatures reacted to the abolitionists by passing laws making it a crime to oppose slavery. Virginia's law, for instance, made it a crime (punishable by up to a year in jail and a $500 fine) to speak or write that owners did not have property rights to slaves; Louisiana even included the death penalty among the possible punishments for anyone tending to promote unrest among slaves.[16]

Sometimes a mob played the part of the censor. Elijah P. Lovejoy brought a printing press to St. Louis, Missouri, and began publishing an antislavery newspaper, the *Observer.* In 1836 a freed slave was accused of attacking two police officers with a knife, and after the judge in the case blamed Lovejoy for stirring up trouble, his newspaper was vandalized three times in one week. When Lovejoy complained that officials would not take action against the vandals, a mob of 200 ransacked his paper, forcing him to move across the Mississippi River to Alton, Illinois, where the *Observer* resumed publication. He was again roundly criticized for his abolitionist views and in 1837 began to fear for his safety. He asked the mayor of Alton to protect his printing press but was rebuffed. Once again, a mob of 200 gathered at Lovejoy's newspaper, ignoring the mayor's call for calm, and soon set fire to the newspaper building. When Lovejoy and another man emerged, Lovejoy was shot five times and killed. No one was ever convicted of the crimes.[17]

Despite the First Amendment, federal censorship of expression was occurring about the same time. A Washington, D.C., doctor was arrested for seditious libel for merely possessing antislavery newspapers, although he was acquitted by a federal jury in 1836 (after he had spent eight months in jail awaiting trial).[18] As the Civil War began, President Lincoln prohibited the mailing of "treasonous" material, and the U.S. postmaster barred several newspapers from the mail.[19] A member of Congress who was opposed to the war, Clement Vallandigham, was arrested for giving a speech in which he called the war "wicked, cruel and unnecessary." He was ordered imprisoned for the duration of the war, but his sentence was commuted and he was banished to live in the Confederacy.[20] E. N. Fuller, publisher of the *Newark Evening Journal* in New Jersey, was arrested and fined in 1864 for allegedly inciting rebellion and discouraging military enlistments by publishing an editorial calling for young men who did not want to be "butchered" to defy Lincoln's draft. O. C. Cone, publisher of New Jersey's *Somerville Messenger* was likewise arrested and fined for reprinting Fuller's editorial.[21]

After the Civil War, one of the duties that the federal government undertook was Reconstruction, in which the devastated Southern states were to reorganize their governments under military supervision and regain their rights as states. One of the more controversial aspects of Reconstruction was the requirement of loyalty oaths. Once 10 percent of a state's citizens signed a loyalty oath pledging allegiance to the federal government and promised to accept the abolition of slavery, the state could be readmitted to the Union. But the first effort at Reconstruction failed because it did not require the states to give rights to former slaves, so another effort at Reconstruction was made, dividing the South into five districts under military control and requiring the states to ratify the 14th Amendment, which was designed to guarantee citizenship rights to former slaves.[22]

Some Southern newspapers rebelled against these requirements. The *Macon (Georgia) Journal and Messenger* was suspended from publication for printing a humorous article about the loyalty oath. The paper in Americus, Georgia, also was suspended. The *Richmond (Virginia) Whig* was suspended, as were papers in Augusta, Georgia, and Salisbury, North Carolina. Editors were arrested in Virginia and Louisiana for criticizing the Reconstruction effort.[23]

The years following the Civil War and Reconstruction, which ended in 1877, were equally perilous times for those who spoke or published dissenting views. During a labor dispute in 1886 in Chicago, someone set off a bomb during a rally at Haymarket Square, killing a police sergeant and injuring 60 other officers; gunfire was then exchanged, killing 10 workers and seven more police officers. Although no one ever determined who ignited the bomb, eight anarchists were tried for murder. Five of them had not even been in Haymarket Square during the melee, but the judge in the case said they had advocated violence with their speech. Seven were sentenced to death: four were executed, one committed suicide, and two were later pardoned by Governor John Peter Altgeld,[24] who said that the men were convicted not for their violent actions but for their vocalized views about American government.[25]

WORLD WAR I AND THE ESPIONAGE ACT

When President William McKinley was assassinated in 1901, a new wave of censorship took hold. New York, New Jersey, and Wisconsin were among the states that enacted laws making it a crime to advocate anarchy.[26] In addition to the anarchists, union organizers were targeted, particularly the Industrial Workers of the World, also called the Wobblies. In the early part of the twentieth century, a number of cities enacted ordinances prohibiting union organizers from speaking, such as one in Los Angeles that made it a crime to "discuss, expound, advocate or oppose" in any city park "the doctrines of any economic or social system." In some cities, Wobblies organizers were arrested en masse and sometimes tortured while in custody. The Wobblies fought for their First Amendment rights in city after city. In one instance in Missoula, Montana, a U.S. Forestry Department employee was watching a free speech debate from his office window, when one man was arrested for reading the Declaration of Independence aloud. Incensed, the Forestry Department worker went downstairs, mounted the platform where the arrest had occurred, and began reading the Declaration of Independence aloud as well; he was also arrested.[27]

As World War I began, members of Congress became concerned about opposition to the war, particularly among socialists, anarchists, and the 25 percent of the U.S. population who were of German descent.[28] In 1917, three weeks after declaring war, Congress passed the Espionage Act, which punished speech that could impede the war effort. The penalty was up to 20 years in prison and a $10,000 fine for interfering with the war effort by promoting the enemies' success, attempting to "cause insubordination, disloyalty, mutiny or refusal of duty," or opposing military enlistment or the draft.[29] Less than a year later, the Espionage Act was amended by the creation of the Sedition Act, which went further than its predecessor by making it a federal crime to "utter, print, write, publish any disloyal, profane, scurrilous or abusive language about the form of government of the United States, or the Constitution of the United States, or the uniform of the Army or Navy."[30] The reasons for the passage of the most restrictive act limiting speech and press since 1798 included widespread opposition to U.S. involvement in the war and the perception of a growing threat from Communists, who in 1917 had overthrown the Russian government in what became known as the Bolshevik Revolution.

Dissent was now a crime, and enforcement was rigid. An Illinois minister, for instance, was imprisoned for preaching that all wars were wrong.[31] A monthly newspaper, *The Masses,* was banned from the mail because of its antiwar cartoons and articles, although that ban was overturned on appeal.[32] A Russian immigrant was sentenced to 10 years in prison for stating during a speech to the Women's Dining Club in Kansas City, Missouri, that "I am for the people and the government is for profiteers," because her speech could been seen as discouraging soldiers and prospective soldiers. The son of the

New Hampshire Supreme Court chief justice was convicted for mailing a letter stating that Germany had promised to end submarine warfare, because the letter could supposedly hurt the draft. Thirty German Americans in South Dakota were convicted after they sent a letter to the governor demanding changes in the selective service draft procedures; their actions were perceived as obstructing the draft. Robert Goldstein, a German immigrant filmmaker, was convicted, and his film, *The Spirit of '76* (1917), seized, because it included a scene in which British soldiers behaved poorly during the Revolutionary War, which the government said reflected badly on Great Britain, America's ally in the war.[33]

One judge who attempted to limit the effect of the Espionage Act was U.S. District Judge Learned Hand. In *Masses Publishing Co. v. Patten,* Hand was asked to rule on a request for an injunction against Postmaster General Albert Burleson, who had banned from the mail the August 1917 issue of *The Masses,* a liberal magazine, because of four poems and four drawings that Burleson said violated the Espionage Act. Hand sided with the magazine, stating in his decision that that the publication did not violate the Espionage Act because it could not be shown to cause opposition to the draft or interfere with the war effort.[34]

Perhaps the most lasting legacy of the Espionage and Sedition acts is the landmark U.S. Supreme Court rulings that stemmed from their enforcement. In the first, Charles Schenck, the general secretary of the Socialist Party, was convicted for distributing 15,000 pamphlets to military recruits and draftees denouncing the draft as unconstitutional. He appealed his conviction, arguing that it violated the First Amendment, but in 1919 the Supreme Court upheld the conviction in *Schenck v. U.S.*[35] The great jurist Oliver Wendell Holmes Jr. wrote the opinion for the Court, writing that the government was justified in prohibiting expression that presents a "clear and present danger" of substantive evil. In language still quoted by many today, Holmes wrote that "the most stringent protection of free speech would not protect a man falsely shouting fire in a theater."[36] Schenck, Holmes wrote, might have been free to express himself during peacetime, but while the nation was at war, his leaflets threatened government.

Later that same year, the Supreme Court was asked to consider again whether speaking out against the war was a crime. In *Debs v. U.S.,* the Supreme Court upheld the conviction of Eugene Debs, national leader of the Socialist Party. Debs, a labor activist who embraced Socialism while imprisoned for a contempt of court charge, had received 900,000 votes when he ran for president in 1912. During a visit to three fellow Socialists in prison in Canton, Ohio, he gave a speech outside the prison, stating, in part, "It is extremely dangerous to exercise the constitutional right of free speech in a country

fighting to make democracy safe in the world.... They tell us that we live in a
great free republic; that our institutions are democratic; that we are a free and
self-governing people. That is too much, even for a joke."[37] He also stated that
"the working class, who furnish the corpses, have never yet had a voice in declaring war."[38] Debs was subsequently arrested for violating the Espionage Act
by obstructing the draft and was sentenced to 10 years in prison. The Supreme
Court rejected Debs's appeal of his conviction, ruling the jury was justified in
finding that Debs's statements would obstruct recruiting.[39]

In yet a third case involving the constitutionality of the Espionage Act,
Jacob Abrams and his codefendants, who were Russian immigrants, were
arrested, convicted, and sentenced to 20 years in prison for distributing two
leaflets, one in English and the other in Yiddish, telling ammunition plant
workers that they were helping to murder Germans and Russians. Again, as
in the earlier *Schenck* and *Debs* cases, the Court upheld the convictions. Although a majority of the Court voted to uphold the convictions, Holmes,
who had written the "clear and present danger" language in *Schenck,* had
apparently had a change of philosophy. He and Justice Louis Brandeis wrote
a dissenting opinion in which they stated they had voted to overturn the
convictions because there was no evidence the defendants' actions repre-
sented a clear and present danger. In a ringing endorsement of the power
of the First Amendment, Holmes wrote, "Prosecution for the expression of
opinions seems to me to be perfectly illogical.... The ultimate good desired
is better reached by the free trade of ideas—that the best test of truth is
the power of the thought to get itself accepted in the competition of the
market."[40]

What led to Holmes's change of heart? First Amendment scholar Geoffrey
Stone cites a chance encounter on a train between Holmes and Judge Hand,
which led to an exchange of letters about their judicial approach. Holmes
also read Zechariah Chafee's influential article in the *Harvard Law Review,*
"Freedom of Speech in War Time," in which Chafee criticized Holmes's rulings in *Schenck* and *Debs* as violating the principles of the First Amendment
protection of free speech. According to Stone, Holmes spent much of 1919
rethinking his approach to free speech, and that led to his dissent in the
Abrams case.[41]

In adopting the language of the marketplace, Holmes was indirectly in-
voking the ideas of English poet John Milton and his 1648 call for freedom
of expression, *Areopagitica*. Rebelling against requirements that all printing be licensed by the government, Milton (who may be better known for
another work, *Paradise Lost*), wrote, "And though all the windes of doctrin
were let loose to play upon the earth, so Truth be in the field, we do in-
juriously by licensing and prohibiting to misdoubt her strength. Let her

and Falsehood grapple; who ever knew truth put to the wors, in a free and open encounter?"[42] Milton was advocating people's right to have access to all points of view on a controversial topic. He was confident the best ideas would win.

Despite Holmes's call for a free and open encounter among competing ideas, his argument did not immediately sway a majority of the Court. But as is sometimes the case, a persuasively written dissenting opinion eventually becomes the majority viewpoint. For example, in another case in 1920, the Court upheld a Minnesota statute making it a crime to argue, orally or in writing, against the draft or military enlistment. The Court upheld the state law in *Gilbert v. Minnesota*,[43] but Brandeis wrote a dissent arguing that the First Amendment applies to state government as well as the federal government. He was in the minority in that case, but just five years later his position became the majority decision in the *Gitlow* case, which applied the First Amendment to the states through the 14th Amendment. This precedent, first articulated in a dissent by Brandeis, had a tremendous impact in 1931, when the Court overturned a Minnesota law allowing officials to shut down a newspaper that was a public nuisance and to allow it to resume publication only upon prior review of a judge. In *Near v. Minnesota,* the Court voted 5–4 to strike down the law as a violation of the First Amendment. Chief Justice Charles Evans Hughes, writing for the majority, noted that our nation fought for its independence from England in part because of prior restraint of the press and that most government attempts to prevent publication of printed material were unconstitutional.[44]

Similarly to how Brandeis's dissent eventually became the Court's majority position, Holmes's dissent in *Abrams* eventually swayed a majority of the Court but not immediately. Congress in 1920 repealed the Sedition Act of 1918, and after 10 years President Franklin Delano Roosevelt granted amnesty to everyone still in prison because of the act.[45]

THE RED SCARE

In the years following World War I, many in positions of power considered Communism the greatest threat to this country; as a result, a number of laws were enacted criminalizing membership in the Communist Party or even association with Communists or Communist sympathizers. The Federal Bureau of Investigation (FBI) began keeping files on suspected Communists and Communist sympathizers in the 1930s, including 2,500 probable subversives. FBI Director J. Edgar Hoover recognized that spying on American citizens would be unpopular if it became public knowledge, saying that investigating political beliefs would be "repugnant to the American people."[46]

This antisubversive movement gained renewed vigor with the United States' entry into World War II following the surprise Japanese attack on Pearl Harbor. President Roosevelt used the FBI to spy on those suspected of disloyalty, ranging from German Americans to Japanese Americans; in addition, the 112,000 Japanese Americans living on the West Coast were forced to relocate to detention centers.[47] All resident aliens, including Japanese, Germans, and Italians, were subject to a curfew beginning in 1942.[48] The FBI investigated average citizens, as well as the press, to ferret out disloyalty. One FBI agent investigating the *Oklahoma City Black Press* found it filled with subversive material, including well-known Communist phrases such as "civil liberties" and "freedom of the press." The FBI also recruited thousands of American Legion members as confidential informants to spy on their neighbors.[49]

The Smith Act, enacted by Congress in 1940, made it a crime to teach or write about the violent overthrow of the government, or to write or speak anything furthering that cause. In addition, mere membership in a group calling for the violent overthrow of the government was a crime, as was organizing the Communist Party.[50] The Supreme Court upheld the constitutionality of the Smith Act in 1951, in *Dennis v. U.S.,* writing that the government was justified in prohibiting expression that could present an internal threat to the nation.[51] The Court's plurality decision read, "Overthrow of the Government by force and violence is certainly a substantial enough interest for the Government to limit speech. Indeed, this is the ultimate value of any society, for if a society cannot protect its very structure from armed internal attack, it must follow that no subordinate value can be protected."[52] In dissents, justices Hugo Black and William O. Douglas argued that free speech, not suppression, was the key to defeating a perceived threat to the nation. Communism, Douglas wrote, "has been so thoroughly exposed in this country that it has been crippled as a political force. Free speech has destroyed it."[53] Black wrote that although public opinion clearly favored enforcement of the Smith Act, eventually in calmer times the Court would use the First Amendment to restore individual rights.[54]

The *Dennis* case was heard during the height of the Cold War, in which fear of Communism led to repeated prosecutions of those who were members of the Communist Party or followers of Communism, leading to charges against an additional 129 people.[55] Perhaps no episode encapsulates the red scare era better than the rise of Senator Joseph McCarthy of Wisconsin. McCarthy rose to prominence with his well-publicized efforts, both on the floor of the Senate and in speeches to outside groups, to root out Communists and Communist sympathizers in the federal government. Innocent people were sometimes smeared by his accusations. His efforts gave rise to the term McCarthyism, referring to the practice of vilifying people while leaving them no recourse to clear their names. McCarthy's methods eventually were called into question, most notably by legendary CBS newsman Edward R. Murrow, as well as by other senators, and he was censured by the Senate.

Another aspect of the red scare was the House Un-American Activities Committee, which was created in 1940. It used its subpoena power and the threat of jail to intimidate those who refused to cooperate and engaged in a hunt for Communists in many areas of American life, notably in the entertainment fields. Those who refused to testify, citing their First Amendment rights to free speech and their Fifth Amendment right against self-incrimination, were blacklisted, essentially making it impossible for anyone to hire them without themselves running afoul of the committee. Approximately 250 people were blacklisted, including noted writers Dorothy Parker, James Thurber, and Arthur Miller.[56] A number of blacklisted screen and television writers were forced to write under assumed names, and some saw their careers ruined as a result of exercising their constitutional rights. Some, like Charlie Chaplin, left the country; others, fearful of losing their careers, caved in and named those whom they believed were Communists or Communist sympathizers, leading to more blacklisting. One of those who refused to cooperate was Academy Award–winning writer Ring Lardner Jr., who went to prison for a year.[57]

Not everyone who was called to testify before the House Un-American Activities Committee declined to testify, though. A number of actors, writers and others in the arts field testified willingly, including actor and future president Ronald Reagan, who was president of the Screen Actors Guild, novelist Ayn Rand, and producers Walt Disney, Louis B. Mayer, and Jack Warner.[58]

It was not only in Washington that efforts were made to eliminate Communism's influence. Forty-two states adopted loyalty oath laws in the wake of the red scare, requiring, for example, that insurance agents (Washington), pharmacists (Texas), and fishing license applicants (New York) had to sign oaths of loyalty to the United States, ignoring the likelihood that anyone seriously intent on undermining the U.S. government would have no problem signing such an oath.[59]

Slowly, the tide began to turn against efforts to punish people for their speech or publications. In 1957, the Supreme Court essentially ended prosecution under the Smith Act in *Yates v. U.S.,* with a majority of the Court making a distinction between "concrete" advocacy of overthrowing the government and the abstract "advocacy or teaching of abstract doctrine."[60] In 1969, the 11th Circuit Court of Appeals in Washington, D.C., ruled in *Boorda v. Subversive Activities Control Board* that the city of Washington violated the First Amendment by punishing a Communist Party member solely for membership in the group: "It seems clear to us that mere membership in the Communist Party is protected by the First Amendment. . . . Therefore the fact that some members of the Communist Party may be engaged in activity not protected by the First Amendment does not mean that the protected activity of other members may be infringed."[61] When the Supreme Court refused to hear an appeal, the lower court's ruling stood.

THE 1960S AND THE VIETNAM WAR

The 1960s and 1970s introduced another form of protest and censorship. U.S. involvement in the Vietnam War brought protesters into the streets. As the military's involvement in the war escalated, opposition began to grow. Those who favored the war complained that the protestors—many with long hair—were hippies intent on destroying the nation. Many protests were disrupted both by police and by bystanders. An October 1967 antiwar march, for instance, sent 50,000 demonstrators to the streets in Washington, D.C. Armed troops used tear gas, rifle butts, and other blunt instruments to attack the protesters, sending 67 to the hospital and 647 to jail; President Lyndon Johnson called the demonstrators part of Communist subversion.[62] Protests aimed at stopping the draft occurred in cities across the country, and in the span of about one year, 250 ROTC (Reserve Officers' Training Corps) buildings were bombed—a rate approaching one a day.[63]

Protests over the Vietnam War erupted at the 1968 Democratic Party Convention in Chicago, when thousands marched in the streets and were attacked by Chicago police. Chanting "the whole world is watching," the demonstrators were beaten and arrested in full view of a national television audience. Seven of the Chicago protest leaders were indicted on charges of crossing state lines to incite a riot and conspiracy to cross state lines to incite a riot. They eventually stood trial in U.S. district court in what became known as the Chicago 7 trial. The trial before U.S. District Judge Julius Hoffman quickly became a circus, with the defendants disrupting the proceedings by waving a Vietcong flag from the defense table and wearing judge's robes to mock Hoffman, who responded by ordering one of the defendants bound and gagged during the trial. The defendants were acquitted of conspiracy, but five were convicted of crossing state lines to incite a riot. Hoffman was disgusted with the defendants and sentenced them to five years in prison, then added jail time for contempt of court for them, the other two defendants, and their lawyers. Eventually, all convictions and contempt citations were overturned on appeal because Hoffman had denied the defendants a fair trial.[64]

The antiwar movement, fueled by President Nixon's announcement that the United States was bombing Cambodia in an apparent escalation of the Vietnam War, turned violent in May 1970, when National Guard members opened fire on an antiwar protest at Kent State University in Ohio, killing four students. A few days after the Kent State shootings, an estimated 1.5 million college students walked out of class, and protesters bombed 30 ROTC buildings on campuses in one week.[65]

The federal government, faced with the largest insurrection since the Civil War, turned to espionage on its own citizens. The FBI, under J. Edgar Hoover, began infiltrating dissident groups and also engaged in widespread warrantless wiretapping, including efforts to disrupt dissident groups by spreading misinformation and encouraging suspicion among members, through COINTELPRO (an acronym for counterintelligence program). The Nixon White House also had the Central Intelligence Agency (CIA) spy on domestic antiwar groups;[66] CIA tactics included illegal break-ins, wiretapping without warrants, and infiltration of antiwar organizations. Even the U.S. Army was involved in spying on domestic groups. The Nixon administration also enlisted the Internal Revenue Service to investigate tax-exempt groups, as well as individuals, and to initiate tax audits of those who opposed the administration's policies. In sum, the Nixon administration engaged in the most aggressive effort to punish dissent ever, surpassing the Adams administration's treatment of opponents with the Sedition Act of 1798 and the pursuit of socialists during the World War I era.

The antiwar movement also led to a landmark Supreme Court ruling on freedom of the press that indirectly led to the unraveling of the Nixon administration's domestic spying program and Nixon's eventual resignation. Daniel Ellsberg was employed by the Rand Corporation, a think tank that had a contract with the U.S. government. While working on classified Defense Department documents, Ellsberg became opposed to U.S. involvement in the Vietnam War. He began secretly photocopying thousands of pages of documents about how the United States had become involved in the war and what actions had been taken in that war effort, then gave copies to both the *New York Times* and the *Washington Post*. Both papers began publishing a series of stories based on these classified documents, called the Pentagon Papers; in response, U.S. Attorney General John Mitchell filed suit in U.S. district court in New York and Washington, seeking an injunction blocking the newspapers from publishing their stories based on stolen classified documents. A U.S. district judge in New York granted an injunction blocking the *Times* stories, but the judge in Washington refused to grant an injunction against the *Post*.

With unprecedented speed, the U.S. Supreme Court took the two cases on immediate appeal, bypassing the normal route through the court of appeals, and issued a ruling just five days later. The Court ruled 6–3 that the government's attempt to block publication of the articles constituted prior restraint and violated the First Amendment. The justices, however, were badly fractured and issued nine separate opinions.[67]

In a development perhaps as significant as the Supreme Court's support for free press, the case helped lead to the Watergate scandal and eventual resignation of President Richard Nixon. White House "plumbers," or secret operatives, broke into the office of Ellsberg's therapist and ransacked his files in an effort to prove Ellsberg was unstable. When the break-in became public, a U.S. district judge dropped criminal charges the Justice Department had filed against Ellsberg for copying and distributing the classified documents, ruling that the government's wrongdoing had corrupted its case against him. The Nixon White House's efforts to cover up this break-in and other criminal acts led to Nixon's resignation in 1974.

Protests against the Vietnam War led to another landmark Supreme Court decision. Back in 1942, the Supreme Court had upheld a New Hampshire state law criminalizing "fighting words," that is, speech so vile that the target's reaction might be to punch the speaker in the nose.[68] In 1971, in *Cohen v. California,* the Supreme Court limited the application of that fighting words doctrine. Paul Robert Cohen had been arrested in Los Angeles Municipal Court for wearing a jacket with the slogan "Fuck the Draft" on the back. He was convicted in superior court of violating California's fighting words law and sentenced to 30 days in jail. The Supreme Court, however, threw out his conviction, ruling that fighting words, rather than being a general political statement, had to be aimed at an individual. Cohen's jacket, the Court ruled, was aimed at a policy not an individual. The threat created by criminalizing Cohen's words, Justice John Marshall Harlan II wrote, was that "governments might soon seize upon the censorship of unpopular ideas as a convenient guise for banning the expression of unpopular ideas."[69]

Unpopular ideas received Supreme Court protection in another case as well, this one involving the Ku Klux Klan. Clarence Brandenburg was a Klan leader who invited a local television station in Cincinnati, Ohio, to attend a cross burning. The television station's film showed Brandenburg giving an inflammatory speech in which he pledged "revenegance" against the group's opponents. He was convicted of violating an Ohio law making it a crime to advocate violence, crime, sabotage, or terrorism as part of a criminal syndicate. The Supreme Court overturned his conviction, however, saying the state could punish speech such as Brandenburg's only if he had called for immediate violent action and if his speech was likely to produce violence.[70]

Together, the *Cohen* and *Brandenburg* decisions demonstrated that the Supreme Court was going to protect unpopular expression, even if the content of that expression was not supported by a majority of the public. As First Amendment scholar Geoffrey Stone writes, "The Court had learned that although each generation's effort to suppress *its* idea of 'dangerous' speech seemed justified at the time, each proved with the benefit of hindsight to have been an overwrought, excessive and dangerous response to the problems facing the nation."[71] That protection for unpopular expression would get perhaps its biggest test in the 1980s.

FLAG BURNING AS A PROTEST

Perhaps the most unpopular expression of an idea that has generated Supreme Court decisions, congressional action, and public controversy is the burning of the American flag in protest. The flag has an important symbolic presence in our nation's history. Our national anthem is a song about the flag, and perhaps the most famous wartime photo ever taken was of World War II soldiers raising the flag on Iwo Jima. For many, particularly veterans, the flag commemorates the struggle for a free country.

An art exhibit in Alaska illustrates the depth of feelings about the flag. An installation at the Visual Arts Center in Anchorage included a piece by the artist Dread Scott titled "What Is the Proper Way to Display a U.S. Flag?" The piece included a comment book for those visiting the arts center to write down their thoughts; however, in order to write in the book, one had to stand on a U.S. flag spread out on the floor. A group of veterans would pay their $5 admission to the show, fold the flag in the traditional triangular shape, then hand it to the museum director along with a book about flag etiquette. The next day, they repeated the exercise, handed the director $50, and took the flag with them. The director had two of the men arrested for misdemeanor theft, and another patron paid to have a new flag placed on the floor. The protest continued, with some people taking the flags and others paying for new flags to replace them.[72]

The flag represents the values that many Americans hold dear, and those intense feelings are what makes protests that include the flag so powerful. Attempts to make flag desecration a crime have run into repeated roadblocks in the courts. The Supreme Court in 1969 overturned conviction of a man for burning a U.S. flag in protest of civil rights violations in the South, ruling that based on the trial court record the justices could not tell whether he was punished for burning the flag or for his comments that occurred at the same time.[73] In 1974, the Supreme Court overturned the conviction of a Washington State college student for showing disrespect for the flag by hanging it upside down in his apartment window with a peace symbol attached to it.[74] Then, in 1989, the Court went further, ruling that a Texas state law making it a crime to desecrate the flag violated the Constitution. In *Texas v. Johnson,* the Court ruled that burning the American flag in protest is symbolic speech protected by the First Amendment.[75] The Court's opinion, written by Justice William Brennan, stated that "if there is a bedrock principle underlying the First Amendment, it is that the government may not prohibit the expression of an idea simply because society finds the idea itself offensive or disagreeable."[76]

Predictably, perhaps, Congress reacted to this decision, first by adopting resolutions condemning the *Texas v. Johnson* decision, then by passing the Flag Protection Act of 1989, which made it a federal crime to mutilate, deface, burn, or otherwise harm the U.S. flag, although it specifically exempted disposal of a U.S. flag when it has become worn or soiled. The next year, ruling on two prosecutions for burning the flag in protest, the Court again ruled that it is a protected expression under the First Amendment.[77] In reaction to this latest Supreme Court decision, members of Congress have repeatedly tried to push through a proposed constitutional amendment banning flag burning, but those efforts have stalled, in one case failing by a single vote in the U.S. Senate in 2006, and no such amendment has yet been enacted.

DISSENT AND PRESIDENTIAL APPEARANCES

More recent government efforts to suppress dissent have taken other forms, most notably as protests over government meetings or even speeches by the president have been forced to take place in isolated "protest pens." When President George W. Bush traveled to a city for a speech, the Secret Service instructed local police to place a protest pen in an area that could not been seen by those in the motorcade, the president, or anyone attending the speech. Any protesters who strayed from the pen or who tried to attend the speech were arrested, although the charges were usually dropped later. This policy of isolating protesters so as not to embarrass the president was challenged in several lawsuits.

The first lawsuit, *ACORN v. Secret Service,* which was heard in U.S. district court in 2003, ended with the Secret Service acknowledging that it could not pen up protesters in isolated areas, and the judge dismissed the suit. The second lawsuit, *ACORN v. Philadelphia,* also in 2003, was dismissed on procedural grounds. A third lawsuit, *Rank v. Jenkins,* was filed in 2004 over the arrest of a Corpus Christi, Texas, couple for their protest during an appearance by President Bush in Charleston, West Virginia. They were arrested for wearing T-shirts that read "Love America, Hate Bush" and "Regime Change Begins at Home." As part of the lawsuit, a manual was discovered in the White House Office of Presidential Advance detailing ways to prevent protesters from attending presidential events and advising the Secret Service to work with local police to restrict protesters to an area "preferably not within view of the event site or motorcade route."[78] Similar protest pens have been used to restrict demonstrators at both the Democratic and Republican conventions in recent years.

THE USA PATRIOT ACT AND TERRORISM

In the wake of the terrorist attacks on 9/11/2001, the patriotism of those who question the federal government's actions has been called into question. When the *New York Times* published a story disclosing a domestic surveillance program initiated under the USA PATRIOT Act, the *Times* was lambasted by the administration, and at least two members of Congress urged that the newspaper and the reporters who wrote the story be charged with treason under the 1917 Espionage Act.[79] In 2003, the Office of Homeland Security sent out a terrorist advisory instructing local police to keep an eye on anyone who "expresses dislike of the attitudes and decisions of the U.S. government."[80]

Supporters contend that the USA PATRIOT Act was necessary to give the government the power to investigate suspected terrorists, allowing agencies such as the FBI and the CIA to share information. Critics contend that the USA PATRIOT Act creates an atmosphere that stifles dissent. For instance, when a 60-year-old man commented at the gym where he exercised that he thought the war in Iraq was more about oil than terrorism, the FBI arrived at his home to question him. A 61-year-old and his son were asked to leave a shopping mall in New York State because they were wearing shirts that said "Peace on Earth" and "Give Peace a Chance." The singing group The Dixie Chicks saw their tapes and CDs destroyed and their radio airtime almost eliminated when they criticized President Bush.[81]

Although the Bush administration did not resort to tactics used in the past, such as the Sedition Act of 1798 or the Espionage Act of 1917, in an effort to stifle dissent, the administration did make it clear how it viewed dissent during the "war on terrorism." Then-Attorney General John Ashcroft, addressing the Senate Judiciary Committee shortly after the 9/11 terrorist attack, equated dissent with aiding the enemy: "To those who scare peace-loving people with phantoms of lost liberty, my message is this: Your tactics only aid terrorists, for they erode our national unity and diminish our resolve. They give ammunition to America's enemies."[82]

CONCLUSION

Despite a culture that espouses support for free speech, U.S. history has been filled with examples of written or spoken dissent punished as a crime, beginning with the Sedition Act of 1798 and continuing through the twenty-first-century fight against terrorism and the USA PATRIOT Act. Forced adherence to the orthodox viewpoint, whether support for the American flag or opposition to Communism, ignores the fact that dissent is at the heart of the American experience. The War of Independence was nothing if not dissent against the government forced on the colonies by the British monarchy. And almost without exception, dissent that arouses official condemnation eventually becomes an accepted, legitimate viewpoint.

Congressman Matthew Lyon, for instance, went to prison for uttering what today would be innocuous criticism of the president, stating, among other things, that the president has "an unbounded thirst for ridiculous pomp, foolish adulation, and selfish avarice."[83] In the twenty-first century, the president is routinely accused of lying. Newspaper editors in the South were arrested for criticizing the federal policy of Reconstruction. Today, the news media are filled with stories questioning federal government actions, and journalists who do so sometimes win awards. During the red scare years, scores went to prison and some were executed merely for being members of groups such as the Communist Party, which today may appear on the ballot on election day. If the history of censorship of dissent teaches anything, it is that dissent is part of American history and part of American life today, and efforts to prevent dissent by punishing expression and limiting First Amendment protections eventually do not succeed.

NOTES

1. John Frohnmayer, *Out of Tune: Listening to the First Amendment* (Nashville, TN: The Freedom Forum First Amendment Center, 1994), 35.

2. William Lowell Putnam, *John Peter Zenger and the Fundamental Freedom* (Jefferson, NC: McFarland, 1997), 115.

3. Although the Zenger verdict had no lasting value as a precedent, it made Zenger's name synonymous with freedom of expression. Even today, groups award the John Peter Zenger Award to First Amendment advocates.

4. Nat Hentoff, *The First Freedom: The Tumultuous History of Free Speech in America* (New York: Delacorte Press, 1980), 62–63. The young Ben Franklin took over publication of the newspaper during his brother's trial and imprisonment.

5. Leonard W. Levy, *Freedom of the Press from Zenger to Jefferson* (New York: Bobbs-Merrill, 1966), xlvi.

6. The First Amendment was actually the third of 12 amendments sent to the states, but because the first two failed to win ratification, the Third Amendment became the First Amendment by default.

7. Douglas M. Fraleigh and Joseph S. Tuman, *Freedom of Speech in the Marketplace of Ideas* (New York: St. Martin's Press, 1997), 71–74.

8. Ibid.

9. Aleine Austin, *Matthew Lyon: "New Man" of the Democratic Revolution, 1749–1822* (University Park: Pennsylvania State University Press, 1981), 108–24.

10. Geoffrey Stone, *Perilous Times: From the Sedition Act of the 1790s to the War on Terrorism* (New York: W. W. Norton, 2004), 54–60.

11. Ibid., 129.

12. Hentoff, *First Freedom,* 84.

13. Levy, *Freedom of the Press,* 366–70.

14. *Gitlow v. New York,* 268 U.S. 652 (1925).

15. Donna Lee Dickerson, *The Course of Tolerance: Freedom of Press in Nineteenth Century America* (New York: Greenwood Press, 1990), 58.

16. Hentoff, *First Freedom,* 89–90.

17. Dickerson, *Course of Tolerance,* 122–25.

18. Ibid., 108–9.

19. Hentoff, *First Freedom,* 93–94.

20. Geoffrey R. Stone, *War and Liberty. An American Dilemma: 1790 to the Present* (New York: W. W. Norton, 2007), 32–39.

21. Hentoff, *First Freedom,* 95–96.

22. Dickerson, *Course of Tolerance,* 202–3.

23. Ibid., 204–5.

24. Hentoff, *First Freedom,* 99–100.

25. Dickerson, *Course of Tolerance,* 227.

26. Hentoff, *First Freedom,* 101.

27. Ibid., 103–5.

28. Stone, *War and Liberty,* 43–44.

29. Hentoff, *First Freedom,* 109–10.

30. Stone, *Perilous Times,* 151.

31. Hentoff, *First Freedom,* 110.

32. Stone, *War and Liberty,* 52–53.

33. Stone, *Perilous Times,* 171–73.

34. 244 F. 536 (S.D. N.Y. 1917).

35. 249 U.S. 47 (1919).

36. Ibid. at 52.

37. Stone, *Perilous Times,* 196–97.

38. Fraleigh and Tuman, *Freedom of Speech,* 95.

39. 249 U.S. 211 (1919).

40. *Abrams v. U.S.,* 249 U.S. 631 (1919).

41. Stone, *Perilous Times,* 200–203.

42. J. Max Patrick, *The Prose of John Milton* (New York: New York University Press, 1968), 327.

43. 254 U.S. 325 (1920).

44. 283 U.S. 697 (1931). The Court said prior restraint still could be constitutional in three situations: the sailing dates of troop ships, incitement to violent overthrow of the government, and obscenity.

45. Stone, *War and Liberty*, 63. The Espionage Act remained in effect.

46. Stone, *Perilous Times*, 249.

47. Jeffrey A. Smith, *War and Press Freedom: The Problem of Prerogative Power* (New York: Oxford University Press, 1999), 20–21. The forced relocation was upheld in the 1944 Supreme Court decision *Korematsu v. U.S.*, 323 U.S. 214 (1944).

48. Stone, *Perilous Times*, 298.

49. Smith, *War and Press Freedom*, 146.

50. Hentoff, *First Freedom*, 137–38.

51. 341 U.S. 494 (1951).

52. Ibid. at 509.

53. Ibid. at 508.

54. Ibid. at 581.

55. Hentoff, *First Freedom*, 145.

56. Stone, *War and Liberty*, 97.

57. Stone, *Perilous Times*, 365–66.

58. Ibid., 360–61.

59. Stone, *War and Liberty*, 98.

60. 354 U.S. 298 (1957) at 319.

61. 421 F.2d 1142 (D.C. Cir. 1969) at 1147–48.

62. Stone, *War and Liberty*, 109.

63. Ibid., 110.

64. Stone, *Perilous Times*, 484–87.

65. Stone, *War and Liberty*, 110.

66. Ibid., 112–13.

67. *New York Times v. U.S.*, 403 U.S. 713 (1971).

68. *Chaplinsky v. New Hampshire*, 315 U.S. 568 (1942).

69. 403 U.S. 15 (1971) at 26.

70. *Brandenburg v. Ohio*, 343 U.S. 444 (1969).

71. Stone, *War and Liberty*, 126.

72. Frohnmayer, *Out of Tune*, 40–45.

73. *Street v. New York*, 394 U.S. 576 (1974).

74. *Spence v. Washington*, 418 U.S. 405 (1974).

75. 497 U.S. 3897 (1989).

76. Ibid. at 414.

77. *U.S. v. Eichman*, 496 U.S. 310 (1990).

78. Matthew Rothschild, "Gagging Protesters by the Manual," *The Progressive*, September 2007, 16.

79. Stone, *War and Liberty*, 155.

80. Jim Hightower, "Bush Zones Go National," *The Nation*, August 16/23, 2004, 29.

81. Jim Cornehls, "The USA PATRIOT Act: The Assault on Civil Liberties," *Z Magazine*, July 2003, 35.

82. Dan Eggen, "Ashcroft Defends Anti-Terrorism Steps: Civil Liberties Groups' Attacks 'Only Aid Terrorists,' Senate Panel Told," *Washington Post*, December 7, 2001.

83. Austin, *Matthew Lyon*, 108.

2

Censorship of the Media during Wartime

Censorship of news reporting during times of war developed during the 1800s, declined in the 1960s and 1970s, then experienced a resurgence in the 1980s. Although there is little doubt that the nation's media face a contradictory mission during times of war—reporting information the public needs to know, while at the same time avoiding reports that threaten the safety of troops in the field—the history of wartime censorship illustrates that military censorship of reporting has often had the primary aim of deflecting news that reflects poorly on those in power.

During the early days of this country, military leaders were little concerned with battlefield reporting because of the tremendous time involved in delivering messages to the newspapers. There was no telegraph, no method of delivering the reports except by horseback and hand delivery. By the time a report of a battle could make it into print, the battle was long over and the troops had moved on to new objectives. There were no war correspondents as we know them today. For example, a reporter's account of the April 19, 1775, battle of Lexington, Massachusetts, believed by many to be the first battle of the Revolutionary War, did not appear in print until May 3 in the *Massachusetts Spy* and not until May 22 in the *New York Gazette*. A relatively current account of the Battle of Long Island, which took place on August 27–29, 1776, appeared in the *Connecticut Courant* on September 2.[1] Nevertheless, military leaders still complained about newspapers. General George Washington, in spring 1777, wrote, "It is much wished that our printers were more discreet in many of their publications. We see in almost every newspaper proclamations or accounts transmitted by the by the enemy of an injurious nature."[2]

THE WAR OF 1812

The Sedition Act of 1798, as detailed in chapter 1, was enacted after the colonies had won their independence and was aimed at critics of the governing party, not at war reporting. In fact, when the fledgling United States declared its first war as a nation, against England in what became known as the War of 1812, the federal government took no steps to establish a similar law, perhaps still smarting from the way the Sedition Act had been used against the minority party; as a result, newspapers were free to editorialize against the war without being prosecuted for sedition.[3] The War of 1812 was not a popular war, with the declaration of war winning approval in the House of Representatives 79–49 and in the Senate 19–13.[4] Newspapers had no organized method of reporting on the war, so that there was no need to institute censorship rules for reporters.[5]

War reports still took time to travel from the battle to the presses, in part because many of the battles took place far from the new nation's population centers. One of the most famous battles of the war, the Battle of New Orleans, ironically took place two weeks after the war had been declared over with the Treaty of Ghent because the delivery of news from Washington was so slow.[6] In one of the first examples of military censorship of the press, General Andrew Jackson, who led the U.S. forces in the Battle of New Orleans, was incensed when the *Louisiana Gazette* reported—accurately, as it turned out—that the peace treaty had been signed and the war was over. Jackson ordered the newspaper to run a retraction, which it did, accompanied by an editor's note that read in part, "We cannot submit to have a censor of the press in our office, and as we are ordered not to publish any remarks without authority, we shall be silent until we can speak with safety."[7]

For the next 30 years, America was at peace. But the Mexican War, which lasted from 1846 to 1848, was fought over 530,000 square miles of land in the Southwest. For the first time, newspapers attempted to provide contemporaneous reports of the fighting. Samuel Morse had invented the telegraph in 1846, and some newspapers used steamships to deliver stories to their printing presses; these new technologies allowed the rapid delivery of news reports from distant sites back to the newspaper office for quick publication, meaning readers at home could keep up-to-date. Some journalists printed single-sided news sheets on the battlefield.[8] Despite these technological developments, however, it still took time for news of some remote battles to reach readers. The *Baltimore Sun* scored a scoop when it printed that Veracruz, Mexico, had fallen; it took 12 days for the news, traveling by Pony Express riders, steamer, and runners, to arrive in Maryland.[9]

THE CIVIL WAR

The Civil War presented new problems for both the press and the military. With the spread of the telegraph, reporting was no longer restricted to hand delivery, and the delays in getting news into print were rapidly disappearing. Coinciding with the spread of the telegraph was the creation of what would become the Associated Press (AP), which relied on reports from journalists throughout the country to provide news to its subscribers.[10] Reporting from the scene of the fighting became commonplace, and the firsthand accounts were riveting to readers at home. For example, a *New York World* reporter watched the shelling of Fort Sumter by rebel forces, marking the beginning of the war.[11]

Donna Dickerson, in her book *The Course of Tolerance: Freedom of the Press in Nineteenth Century America,* writes that censorship of the press took three forms during the Civil War: arrest of correspondents and/or expulsion from the front, censorship of communication via the telegraph or mail, and suppression of newspapers.[12] All three forms were used both in the North and in the South, but perhaps no one was more adept at or more vigorous about censoring the press than famed Union General William Tecumseh Sherman.

Sherman had a long-lived distrust of reporters and often thought their actions were aimed at undermining his authority or helping the Southern forces he was fighting against. Throughout the Civil War, Sherman did whatever he could to eliminate press coverage of his military campaigns, writing in one letter that Civil War correspondents were "dirty newspaper scribblers who have the impudence of Satan" and calling them "spies and defamers" and "infamous lying dogs."[13] Sherman is said to have reacted with joy when told that three reporters had been killed by an exploding shell: "Good. Now we'll have news from hell before breakfast."[14]

Sherman's animosity toward the press can be traced to early reporting about the war. The *Cincinnati Commercial* reported on Sherman's appearance at Lebanon Junction, 26 miles from Louisville: his uniform was too small and he had the appearance of someone who had "suddenly tumbled out ten minutes too late for train."[15] Worse, the rumor that Sherman was mentally unbalanced appeared in several newspapers, including the *New York Tribune,* the *New York Times,* and the *Cincinnati Commercial,* which published the blunt headline "General William T. Sherman Is Insane."[16] The story in the *Commercial* was especially damning: "Gen. William T. Sherman, late commander of the Department of the Cumberland, is insane. It appears that he was at the time while commanding in Kentucky, stark mad."[17]

Based on this reporting, it should be no surprise that Sherman placed severe restrictions on the press. When he left Memphis for Vicksburg in December 1862, he issued an order that anyone "found making reports for publication which might reach the enemy giving them information and comfort, will be arrested and treated as spies."[18] That order was tested by Thomas Knox, a reporter for the *New York Herald.* Knox reported on the siege of Vicksburg, which ended in defeat for the Union forces, and wrote an article commenting not only on the military conflict but also on Sherman's fitness for command, writing, "General Sherman was so exceedingly erratic that the discussion of the past twelve months with respect to his sanity, was revived with much earnestness."[19] Sherman reacted by accusing Knox of publishing military information that would allow the Confederate army to know within 1,000 soldiers how many troops Sherman had at his disposal, even though Knox's account did not appear in print for three weeks. Sherman charged him with being a spy and convened a court martial to try Knox; he was found not guilty of spying, but a jury did find that he had disobeyed Sherman's orders and banished him from the front.[20]

Although the press's treatment of Sherman and Sherman's treatment of the press are among the best-known incidents involving newspapers and the Civil War, they were by no means unique. When troops from Massachusetts marching through Washington, D.C., at the start of the war became involved in a riot with Southern sympathizers, Secretary of State William H. Seward prohibited newspapers from publishing the names of the dead and wounded and placed a censor in the city's telegraph office so that news of the melee would not get out.[21]

Union General Winfield Scott issued an order in 1862 banning any military information from the telegraph lines unless he personally approved the transmission, although he later amended the order to allow newspaper correspondents to transmit stories about battles that had already been fought. That amended order went by the wayside, however, when the Union army was defeated at the first Battle of Bull Run in Virginia; General Scott ordered the Washington telegraph office closed to prevent dissemination of news about the defeat. A week later, General George McClellan issued a new order banning all communications about military affairs, including troop movements, without McClellan's personal approval; violations could bring the death penalty.[22]

Scattered censorship of reporters continued throughout the war. For instance, when the Union army began massing in the Washington area to prepare for a march on the Confederate capital of Richmond, Virginia, Secretary of War Edwin Stanton revoked all press passes and ordered reporters to leave the area, and several reporters were arrested.[23] McClellan, waging a long battle against Confederate General Robert E. Lee, banned correspondents from reporting about the campaign, and the editor of the *Baltimore American* was arrested for reporting about McClellan's forces and about a private conversation the editor had had with President Lincoln.[24]

The government in Washington also took steps to rein in the press, particularly border-state newspapers that promoted secessionism or urged a quick end to war; it shut down as many as 300 papers during the Civil War.[25] Several newspapers were banned from the mail because they opposed the war; most were edited by Democrats who opposed Lincoln's Republican administration.[26] The editor of the *New York Daily News,* Benjamin Wood, and one of his correspondents were arrested for supporting secession, and the paper was ordered closed by Secretary Stanton. Similarly, the mailing privileges of two German-language newspapers were revoked at the suggestion of a grand jury.[27] Union soldiers destroyed the *Columbus (Ohio) Crisis* in March 1863, and two months later the military government of Missouri banned the sale of a number of newspapers; in addition, General Ambrose Burnside suppressed the *Chicago Times* and prohibited the *New York World* from being sold in Ohio.

At times, military leaders censored the press because of criticism of their actions. General John Charles Fremont had the editor of the *St. Louis Evening News* arrested and the newspaper office seized after it printed an article blaming him for the Union army's defeat at Lexington, Missouri. In New Orleans, Major General Benjamin Butler, upon taking control of the Southern city, issued a series of orders prohibiting signs of disrespect for his soldiers or his command. One order stated that any women who "by gesture or movement insult, or show contempt" for Union soldiers or officers would be treated as prostitutes. When the New Orleans papers refused to print the order, Butler ordered them closed.[28]

Some newspaper editors supported the military's censorship rules. The *Cincinnati Daily Gazette* wrote that the military had a duty to suppress information that might be helpful to the enemy and that "in times of war, the press must concede a portion of its rights and interests to the common good."[29] The *New York Times* wrote that the temporary suspension of the "minor" rights such as the freedom of the press "is a small price to pay for their permanent and perpetual enjoyment."[30] Others acknowledged the need to restrict the transmission of some information over the telegraph wires but urged the government to appoint censors who would use common sense, rather than instituting a blanket ban on war information.

But some editors objected to the idea that newspapers could be censored in cities in the North where there was no fighting. Famous *New York Tribune* editor Horace Greeley called a meeting of New York newspaper editors in the wake of Burnside's seizure of the Chicago paper. They agreed that in times of war, although no journalist should be allowed to publish incitement to rebellion or treason, any limits on a free press "should be confined to localities wherein hostilities actually exist or are imminently threatened." Burnside eventually rescinded his order.[31]

In the South, little censorship of the press occurred because there was little printed dissent against the Confederacy. Most editors who opposed the war simply sold the papers and left the South. For instance, in 1860, while talk of secession was in the air, two abolitionists were hanged in Fort Worth, Texas; when a grand jury in a neighboring county recommended that the editor of the *Fort Worth Chief* be treated the same way, he took the hint and sold his paper to a secessionist.[32] One who did not sell was the editor of the *Galveston (Texas) Union,* who advocated caution in the war and saw his paper's offices trashed by a mob. One editor who did run into censorship by the Confederate government was William G. Brownlow, who published the *Whig* in Knoxville, Tennessee. Brownlow, who supported slavery but opposed secession by the Southern states, was charged with treason and, when he refused to swear loyalty to the Confederacy, also with sabotage. Sentenced to jail, he escaped, was captured in North Carolina and brought back to Knoxville, went to jail, and eventually was banished in 1863 to live in the North. Ironically, when the Union seized Knoxville in 1864, Brownlow returned, reopened his newspaper, and eventually was elected governor of Tennessee in 1865 and again in 1867, then was elected to represent Tennessee in the U.S. Senate in 1869.[33]

THE SPANISH-AMERICAN WAR

Although censorship of the press had become commonplace during the Civil War, the Spanish-American War, which began in 1898 over perceived aggression by Spain in the Caribbean, brought more restrictions for reporters because delivery of correspondents' accounts and subsequent publication in newspapers was much faster than during the Civil War, with a telegraph dispatch from Santiago, Cuba, to Washington taking just 20 minutes.[34] In addition, the Civil War had taken place mainly in the eastern United States, giving newspaper correspondents relatively easy access to the site of fighting. The Spanish-American War, in contrast, took place primarily in Cuba, accessible only by sea and only with the cooperation of military leaders. When a reporter asked to go ashore with the first U.S. troops heading into Cuba, General William Shaffer responded, "I don't give a damn who you are."[35] Telegraph messages from Key West and Tampa, Florida, were censored, not only to prevent newspapers from printing information the enemy could use, but also to search for messages from Spanish agents. For the first time, a former reporter, Lieutenant Grant Squires, who had worked at the *New York Tribune,* was named the chief telegraph censor in New York.[36] Hiring former journalists to be wartime censors was an idea that would prove popular for the government in twentieth-century conflicts.

Telegraph censorship was pronounced. Telegraph operators were functioning under censorship orders and sometimes would censor news stories based on their own interpretations, including a nearly total block of reporting from Key West.[37] Admiral William Sampson cut the underwater telegraph line from Havana to Key West to prevent reporters from getting their stories to their publications.[38] But some reporters had their own boats, accompanying U.S. troop ships as they arrived in Cuba, bypassing some censorship efforts.[39] Telegraph transmission of news by reporters was given the lowest priority, and some correspondents were limited to transmitting no more than 100 words a day.[40]

Another trend that continued from the Civil War was censorship for purely public relations or public opinion purposes. When the war spread to the Philippines and the United States took control of the island nation from Spain, Elwell S. Otis, the military commander and governor general, told his censor in Manila "to let nothing go that can hurt the administration." When journalists complained that his censorship was turning their reporting into pro-American propaganda, he threatened them with court martial for conspiracy against the government.[41]

Many of the efforts to censor the press failed, however, both because the sheer number of reporters overwhelmed the small number of censors and because political leaders in Washington, seeking to win public support for a war that was not overwhelmingly popular, were more interested in having news of battlefield successes published than they were in restricting what newspapers could publish.[42] After the war, Squires argued that censorship of the press had been minimal, and Brigadier General A. W. Greeley wrote that reports of severe censorship during the Spanish-American War were "entirely unfounded."[43]

WORLD WAR I

Censorship of the press continued when the United States entered World War I in Europe. As recounted in chapter 1, the federal government used the Espionage Act of 1917 and the Sedition Act of 1918 to quash dissent at home, including opposition to the war or the draft. But the Espionage Act presented to Congress included a provision that made it a crime to publish information that the president decided might be useful to the enemy. This provision brought objections from the press, including the American Newspaper Publishers' Association, and the House of Representatives narrowly defeated it 188–144.[44]

Censorship of the news media began even before the United States entered the war. As early as 1914, while the United States was still proclaiming neutrality in the growing European war, President Woodrow Wilson issued an executive order banning radio stations from broadcasting anything about the war that was not neutral, and the navy assumed control of long-distance radio stations on the Atlantic Coast, relying on an attorney general's opinion that the president had broad power to "preserve the integrity of the United States."[45] Few newspapers took note of the increasing number of censorship laws. As historian James Mock put it, "So engrossing to Americans was the world scene during World War I that, apparently, they were never aware of piece after piece of federal legislation which, when fitted together, made the mosaic of censorship."[46]

As the war effort began in the United States, President Wilson created a Committee on Public Information, which had the dual role of using public relations techniques to drum up support for the war and of imposing a system of voluntary self-censorship on the press, including limits on the publication of troops' sailing dates. In addition, the committee ruled that all photographs or motion picture films about the war had to gain prior approval. George Creel, a journalist and public relations expert, was placed in charge of the committee.[47] Some press members criticized Creel's committee for its censorship efforts, but there was no widespread opposition to the committee's actions, with 99 percent of the nation's newspapers following the self-censorship guidelines, which left it to the newspapers to police their own content and whether it complied with the Creel committee's guidelines.[48]

Once the United States gave up its neutrality and entered the war in 1917, the Wilson administration took swift action, giving the War Department the authority to censor telegraph and telephone lines and giving the navy censorship control over undersea cables.[49] The president also established a Censorship Board, made up of the secretaries of war and the navy, the postmaster general, the War Trade Board, and Creel as head of the Committee on Public Information. Newspapers, preoccupied with the World Series and other news, paid little attention.[50] During the war, the post office denied mailing privileges to more than 400 issues of newspapers and magazines because their content was seen as interfering with the war effort.[51]

Censorship was the rule for journalists wanting to cover the fighting. In order to report from Europe, reporters had to undergo a lengthy accreditation process, including an appearance before the War Secretary, and post a $10,000 bond that would be forfeited if they violated the rules.[52] Once at the front in Europe, reporters had to wear uniforms and submit their stories to army censors. Stories could not mention the names or locations of army units, and reporters were forbidden to do anything that might harm the troops' morale. A statement of censorship principles issued in 1918 made it clear that, in addition to protecting the troops, one of its purposes was public relations: stories had to be accurate, not provide information to the enemy, not harm morale, and not embarrass the United States. At least four reporters either voluntarily left the front to protest the draconian censorship or had their credentials revoked for violating the rules, but almost all journalists complied.[53]

In at least one instance, press reports were censored because the news reflected incompetence by those in power, not because military secrets were disclosed. When the secretaries of war and the navy denied reports that military recruits were not receiving needed supplies and equipment—they were getting shipments of lawn mowers and floor wax but not food or clothing—General John Pershing asked that censors allow newspaper stories about the problem to be published, but the Censorship Board refused. The news still got out when reporters wrote letters to former president Teddy Roosevelt, who forwarded the complaints to a Philadelphia newspaper, which then published the stories without having to go through military censors.[54]

For the first time in a U.S. war, the new medium of film was subjected to censorship. The *Exhibitor's Trade Review,* a publication targeting theater owners, acknowledged the need to be careful what films they showed to ensure public support for the government: "Any influence which tends to rob the government, of that support, or to weaken it, could properly and would undoubtedly be put down. This is true of any other medium of expression as it is of motion pictures. But it is particularly true of the motion picture."[55]

In a continuation of the practice that began in the Spanish-American War, a former journalist, Frederick Palmer, was named as the army's chief censor in Europe, admitting after the war that he had been a "public liar to keep up the spirit of the armies and the peoples of our side."[56] Even mail home from soldiers was subject to review and censorship, with soldiers told as soon as they entered basic training what they could write and whom they could write to. They also were forbidden to serve as paid correspondents for any publication.[57] All censorship, including voluntary censorship, ended with the conclusion of the war.

WORLD WAR II

Whereas U.S. involvement in World War I came about slowly, World War II, while already under way in Europe, came suddenly to the United States when the Japanese military attacked Pearl Harbor on December 7, 1941. News of the scale of the attack was withheld from the media so that the Japanese would not know how the attack had devastated the U.S. Navy; release of photographs and newsreel footage showing some of the 2,400 deaths was delayed by two years, and news about the damage to ships was delayed for a year until some of the damaged vessels could be repaired and put out to sea. Columnist Drew Pearson, when he tried to publish details of the attack, was rebuked by the director of the Federal Bureau of Investigation (FBI), J. Edgar Hoover, who told him he was being unpatriotic. Consequently, Pearson decided not to publish the material.[58] Although some of the censorship of news about the Pearl Harbor attack was aimed at keeping the information out of Japanese hands, it also was aimed at limiting the embarrassing news that the United States had fallen victim to a surprise attack that military officials might have seen coming.

Almost immediately after the attack on Pearl Harbor, President Franklin Delano Roosevelt created the Office of Censorship, which imposed voluntary censorship on the American news media and official censorship on international communication coming out of the United States. Continuing the practice developed during the previous war, the Office of Censorship was headed by Byron Price, an Associated Press newsman for 29 years, and executive editor of the wire service.

If the Civil War was the first "telegraph" war, then World War II was the first "radio" war, with the new medium playing an important role in disseminating information to the public. Although commercial radio had been in its infancy during World War I, by 1926 there were 900 radio stations in America, prompting Congress to create the Federal Radio Commission in 1927 and then the Federal Communications Commission (FCC) in 1934 to regulate radio. Therefore, military orders concerning the media took into account both print and radio. The Office of Censorship, for example, asked radio stations to stop giving weather forecasts over the air because the German navy could use the information in its submarine campaign against U.S. shipping.[59] In one bizarre event, a radio broadcast of a 1942 football game between the Chicago Bears and a college all-star team could not mention that the field was enshrouded in fog so thick that the announcers in the booth could not even see the field.[60] Four months after Pearl Harbor, the Justice Department ruled that the Office of Censorship had complete control over all radio, ranging from small transmitters used by employers to the 900 commercial radio stations.[61]

The Office of Censorship attempted to develop a censorship guideline that editors and broadcasters could follow, and in 1942, just a few months after Pearl Harbor, the office distributed 50,000 copies of its Code of Wartime

Practices, then sent out 70,000 copies of a revised code in mid-1942. But when the Office of Censorship learned that many editors either had not read the document or did not understand it, the office recruited newspaper editors to serve as an informal committee to make sure every editor had a copy of the censorship guidelines and understood them.[62] The post office and the FBI monitored the print media for signs of subversive content, and the mailing privileges of four publications were revoked because of their political content. Most newspapers, however, abided by the voluntary self-censorship, including prohibitions on publishing details about the movements of President Roosevelt or other important figures. For example, newspapers did not report that British Prime Minister Winston Churchill was traveling to America in December 1941, two weeks after Pearl Harbor, because of fears the Germans would target his ship as it sailed through the submarine-infested Atlantic.[63] Likewise, newspapers kept quiet when Roosevelt traveled in his bulletproof railcar on a two-week, 8,754-mile tour of defense plants, even though many in the public saw him and knew he was traveling.[64]

In 1942, President Roosevelt created a second wartime information agency, the Office of War Information (OWI), headed by broadcast journalist Elmer Davis, to regulate and release information coming out of the military and the federal government, an effort to separate the censorship of media and the release of propaganda and information from the military into separate agencies and avoid some of the problems associated with the Creel committee's efforts in World War I. The Office of War Information also served as a public relations tool promoting the Roosevelt presidency.[65] The Office of Censorship and the OWI drafted a five-page agreement on the censorship duties of both, and both continued to engage in varying levels of censorship. The OWI included a film censorship division, which reviewed scripts and film content,[66] and also assumed control of shortwave radio transmitters.[67] The OWI was headed on an alternating basis by three newspaper editors or publishers— Garner Cowles Jr. of the *Des Moines Register* and several other publications, E. Palmer Hoyt of the *Portland Oregonian,* and George W. Healy Jr. of the *New Orleans Times-Picayune.*

More journalists covered World War II in Europe and the Pacific than had covered any of the country's previous wars, with 1,646 accredited journalists and as many as 500 war correspondents covering the fighting at any one time.[68] As in World War I, war correspondents covering the fighting had to wear military uniforms with a "C" stitched on the sleeve. A few correspondents, most notably United Press correspondent and later CBS news anchor Walter Cronkite, flew on air force planes conducting bombing raids and were trained to fire weapons at enemy aircraft, even though the Geneva Conventions forbid civilian journalists from carrying weapons because if they were captured, they faced execution. As Cronkite tells the story, "Apparently, the Air Force considered, rationally enough, that once you bailed out of an airplane, the enemy could scarcely know whether you had fired a gun or not. And they figured that we might as well be able to take the place of wounded gunners."[69] In fact, Cronkite was assigned a gunner's spot on flights he took and did fire at German aircraft.[70] Cronkite was not alone in reporting from the front. During the D-Day invasion of France, 27 reporters accompanied the troops.[71]

Bad news from the battlefield rarely made it past censors; neither did stories about looting, shooting of unarmed prisoners, or even about reverses suffered by Allied troops. Many journalists willingly went along with the notion that bad news would harm morale at home and at the front. As Cronkite's successor as CBS news anchor, Dan Rather, put it, "When it came to the overall purpose of the war, the US correspondents (and their Allied counterparts) were no less committed to the defeat of Nazi Germany and Imperial Japan than were the commanders who led their troops into battle."[72]

Even news of peace was controlled. When the war in Europe ended with Germany's surrender, the army issued an embargo—a prohibition against reporting—on news of the armistice until Russian troops could enter Berlin and announce the end of the European war at the same time. An AP reporter, Edward Kennedy, broke the embargo after witnessing the signing of the peace treaty, and the AP broke the news. Brigadier General Frank Allen, head of the Supreme Allied Command's Public Relations Division, responded by suspending the AP's operations in Europe for eight hours, and the AP fired Kennedy.[73]

Among the best-kept secrets throughout the war, at least to the American public, were the Manhattan project and the development of the atomic bomb. An entire city was created in eastern Tennessee, Oak Ridge, whose existence was never reported, nor was the development and testing of the bomb in New Mexico. The subsequent bombing of the Japanese cities of Hiroshima and Nagasaki came as a surprise to the U.S. public. Even after the bombings, news about the blasts were strictly controlled; film footage of the devastation was confiscated, and reporters were prohibited from revealing the harm caused by radiation. Even after the war ended, the press and radio broadcasters were urged not to discuss the atomic bomb without first receiving official approval from the War Department.[74]

THE COLD WAR AND KOREA

The end of World War II in Europe and the Pacific brought with it a new kind of conflict, not fought on the battlefield but waged between the two superpowers that emerged from the war, the United States and the Union of Soviet Socialist Republics (which eventually dissolved in 1991). Relations between the two countries, strained ever since the Bolsheviks overthrew the czar in 1917 and gained control of Russia, suffered further harm in the years after World War II when it became clear that Russian intelligence had learned how the United States manufactured atomic weapons. President Harry Truman, who had succeeded the late President Roosevelt and oversaw the final days of victory in World War II, made provisions for reimposing military censorship if the United States were to go to war with the Soviet Union.[75]

However, it was not against the Soviet Union that America next went to war. Instead, U.S. military forces next took to the battlefield in Korea, beginning in 1950, and the eventual opponent was China. General Douglas MacArthur, who was in charge of the U.S. forces in Korea, as well as the military of U.S. allies, initially proclaimed that he opposed censorship, although he did support voluntary censorship of reports that might aid the enemy. MacArthur even reinstated several correspondents who were expelled from Korea for reports that Lieutenant General Walton Walker, in charge of the ground troops, said aided the enemy. When President Truman and the new Defense Secretary, George C. Marshall, urged MacArthur to impose censorship because of the news reports coming out of Korea, MacArthur finally agreed, and the Eighth Army in Korea imposed its own censorship rules on reporters.

Some of the censorship rules were intended to ensure that reporters did not write negative articles. Stories could be censored if they revealed sensitive information, embarrassed the United States or its allies (even neutral countries), or harmed troop morale. Reporters, although not in uniform as they had been in World War II, were still under military control and faced possible court martial if they violated the rules.[76]

During the peace talks between North and South Korea that eventually led to a truce, the censorship became almost complete. Reporters assigned to the United Nations Command were not permitted to talk to negotiators, and they were briefed hours after the negotiation sessions by an army officer who had not even attended the negotiations. Even the news that was spoon-fed to reporters was often false or misleading, casting the North Koreans as unwilling to compromise.[77] As the talks continued, several correspondents were exiled to Tokyo and labeled as "Reds" because they had reported details of the talks.[78] News of a riot by prisoners at a United Nations prison camp and the seizure of the American commander by prisoners at another camp was withheld by the military, although both stories still eventually made it into print.[79]

Unlike World War II, there was no official censorship in the United States, either voluntary or mandatory. The press and broadcasters were free to report what they liked, although the information coming out of Korea was heavily censored. That may have been because almost every mainstream newspaper initially supported U.S. involvement in Korea.[80] Before, during, and after the war, however, efforts were made to ensure that newspapers and broadcasters toed the line and did not allow "subversive" content to endanger the political will of the public. The Senate Internal Security Subcommittee, with Senator James Eastland of Mississippi as chair, was assigned the job of detecting subversion and infiltration by those who sought the violent overthrow of the government. The committee called approximately 20 journalists to testify during 1954, as well as leaders of the newspaper workers' union, the American Newspaper Guild. Several journalists lost their jobs either because they acknowledged to the subcommittee that they had once had Communist affiliations or, in the case of a *New York Times* reporter, because he refused to testify, citing his Fifth Amendment right not to be forced to testify against himself. Then in 1958, 38 more journalists were subpoenaed by the subcommittee, but the subcommittee never succeeded in finding any high-profile subversives.[81]

VIETNAM

Reporters covering wars were subject to censorship during previous twentieth-century wars, but the Vietnam War was different. The news media faced few restrictions on where they went and what they reported. Indeed, Vietnam was the first war in which the news media did not see their primary role as serving the war effort.[82] News reporters, including television crews, were free to hitch rides with whatever military unit was heading to a location where the journalists thought there would be some action, with only a few voluntary guidelines. There was no centralized censorship mechanism, as there had been in the previous wars; instead, the military attempted to control the release of information by holding regular briefings for the media. The media responded by largely ignoring or openly ridiculing the officers giving the briefings, which were called the "five o'clock follies."

One reason for the lack of censorship was that the Kennedy administration, which had been responsible for expanding the U.S. military presence in Vietnam, insisted that no war was taking place in the Southeast Asian country, and if there was no war, there was no need for military censorship. Many of the midlevel officers became disenchanted with the U.S. war effort and freely shared their pessimistic views with the reporters in the field.[83]

The White House attempted to rein in the press in Vietnam by putting pressure on news executives at home. President Kennedy, in a meeting with *New York Times* publisher Arthur Ochs Sulzberger Sr., asked whether the *Times* had thought about transferring one of its high-profile correspondents,

David Halberstam, from Vietnam. Sulzberger replied that he was happy with Halberstam; he then canceled a planned vacation for the reporter so that the Kennedy administration would not think its pressure had worked. Similarly, President Lyndon Johnson asked the Associated Press's personnel chief at lunch one day whether its reporter in Vietnam, Peter Arnett, had been in Vietnam too long. *New York Times* writer Harrison Salisbury, who even traveled to North Vietnam and reported on the ineffectiveness of U.S. bombing there, was investigated by the FBI to see whether he was a Communist. When CBS correspondent Morley Safer filmed U.S. Marines burning huts in a village, Johnson falsely accused him of being a Communist and told CBS President Frank Stanton that the network was unpatriotic, threatening to go public with its information about Safer's political affiliations unless he was fired. CBS did not give in to the president's demand and Safer was not fired.[84]

The emphasis the White House placed on Safer's visual images from the war highlights the fact that the Vietnam War was the first war covered by television journalists, a development made possible both by the fact that most American homes had television sets and by technological developments that made it easy to carry equipment in the field and to get film back to be aired by the three major networks, NBC, CBS, and ABC. Many people believe that graphic footage of wounded and dead soldiers, broadcast into the public's living rooms night after night, persuaded a growing number of people to oppose the war. Studies of newscast content, however, illustrate that the belief of graphic television footage is not accurate. One study found that 22 percent of the television news coverage of Vietnam before the 1968 Tet Offensive depicted battle scenes,[85] and another study showed that just 3 percent of the footage from Vietnam showed "heavy" fighting.[86] Before the Tet Offensive (which marked the turning of public opinion in the United States against the war when the Vietcong attacked deep inside South Vietnam at a time when the U.S. military claimed it was winning the war), only 16 of 167 television news clips had more than one image of dead or injured.[87] Furthermore, claims that unvarnished television coverage showing blood and death prompted a change in public opinion are disputed in another study, which showed that the decline in public support for the Korean War, where there was censorship and no television coverage, and the decline for support for the Vietnam War, where there was television coverage and no official censorship, occurred at the same rate.[88] Historian Andrew Huebner writes that television and print coverage of the war was much more complex than suggested by critics' image of a hostile media that undermined public support for the military support:

Despite the usefulness of such interpretations, the common implication that Tet was a turning point in news coverage—as well as the emphasis on journalists' commitment to the war effort before it—may obscure the fact that troubling images of American GIs did circulate in the media early in the Vietnam War. News from Vietnam between 1965 and 1968 presented the war as anything but a "romantic adventure." Although the mainstream press was not explicitly "antiwar" before Tet, it did lay bare the confusion, misery, difficulty, and tragedy of the conflict. At the same time, though, the media did not merely sensationalize the war through constant blood and gore. Early coverage of the Vietnam War on television and in popular periodicals was enormously complex, at times foreshadowing the grim and critical reporting of the post-Tet years.[89]

Military leaders, including the U.S. commander General William Westmoreland, pointed to television coverage of the Tet Offensive, which was a defeat for the Vietcong but was framed as a defeat for the United States because the Vietcong briefly occupied the U.S. Embassy in Saigon, as affecting public perceptions about the war.[90] The war also marked an end to the military–press relationship in which both saw their role as supporting the troops. Instead, the Vietnam War marked the beginning of mistrust that poisoned the military–press relationship, breeding skepticism on the part of the press and suspicion on the part of the military.

As the war continued, television coverage began to shift, echoing the public's growing opposition. One study shows that from the Tet Offensive until 1972, the number of times that casualties were shown on television increased, with the biggest increase for casualties among Vietnam civilians.[91] By the time Richard Nixon succeeded Lyndon Johnson as president in 1969, it was clear to many people in and outside the government that the U.S. war effort in Vietnam was doomed.

GRENADA, PANAMA, AND THE PRESS POOL

Despite evidence to the contrary, many in the federal government, particularly in the Pentagon, came to believe that the media, particularly television, had cost the United States victory in Vietnam, that journalists were the reason the military withdrew before defeating the Vietcong. William Hammond, a military historian, says U.S. military officers in Vietnam expected the same deference from the media that their predecessors in every war since the Civil War had received. Instead, many of the journalists were skeptical. "In the end," Hammond writes, "the war itself—rather than the press or the perceived failure of the government to adequately prepare for war—alienated the American public. Every time the number of Americans killed or wounded increased by a factor of 10—going from 1,000 to 10,000, from 10,000 to 100,000—public support as measured by the Gallup Poll fell by 15 percentage points."[92]

By the time the Reagan presidency began in 1980, many of the midlevel military officers who had served in Vietnam had become high-ranking Pentagon officials able to make military policy, and many of them harbored ill will toward the media stemming from their time in Southeast Asia. Their ascension to power meant that the next time the United States took military action, the press would have to abide by new rules.

In 1983, the United States, concerned because of perceived Cuban influence in the tiny Caribbean island nation of Grenada and the threat to American students attending a medical school there, invaded the country. It took just three days to achieve military victory, but firsthand reports of the fighting never reached the America public; for the first time in the nation's history, journalists were not allowed to witness most of the fighting. President Reagan said the exclusion of the media was needed to ensure the surprise element of the invasion, even though the news media in Grenada and elsewhere in the region had predicted the attack.[93] The decision to bar the press was widely supported by top military officials, still smarting over the perceived influence of television reporters in Vietnam.

More than merely being banned from the island, reporters attempting to arrive at Grenada by chartered boat actually came under fire from navy ships under the order of Vice Admiral Joseph Metcalf II, who said that his primary mission was to protect the troops and that he had no interest in protecting the First Amendment.[94] The news media were not allowed on the island until the third day, when a few mop-up actions were still going on but the bulk of the brief war was over.[95]

The decision to block reporters from the fighting was widely criticized both in Congress and in the nation's newspapers. The *New York Times* editorialized that the decision prevented the American public from knowing what was going on, and CBS anchor Walter Cronkite scoffed at the idea that the decision was made to protect reporters' lives. Despite media complaints, public opinion polls supported the decision to bar reporters from the battlefield.[96]

The chairman of the Joint Chiefs of Staff, in an attempt to end the growing media complaints, formed a committee headed by a retired general to create a workable plan for allowing the media to cover future conflicts. The Sidle Commission, named after its chair, developed a plan to create press pools to cover the initial fighting. A press pool, which was not a new idea, is a way to allow a representative from various types of media to cover an event, such as a trip by the president; the press pool members' job is to document any news that occurs and then provide copies of their reports to other media members who were not in the pool.

Under the Sidle plan, a press pool of 16 members representing all forms of news media would be notified when a military action was about to begin.

The plan called for this pool to be taken to the scene to provide a firsthand account of the fighting, and the rest of the media would be allowed to send representatives after the first three days of fighting. The plan was designed to ensure the secrecy of the military plans while still allowing limited press coverage. The first two times the pool was activated—for the bombing of Libya and escorting oil tankers through the Persian Gulf—the process worked well.

But the pool system collapsed during the next major U.S. military action, the invasion of Panama in 1989 to arrest Panamanian leader Manuel Noriega. Secretary of Defense Dick Cheney (who later became vice president) ordered the pool to be activated too late for the media to arrive before the fighting started, and when they did arrive in Panama, the members were taken to non-fighting events, such as the arrival of the U.S. ambassador. In addition, special operations soldiers were told not to talk to the press. Even when journalists were taken to "hot zones," they were forbidden to take pictures or video of wounded soldiers, and the written accounts by wire service and print reporters were delayed because there was no working fax and the commanding officer refused to let them dictate their stories over the phone. Cheney later acknowledged he made a conscious decision, in an effort to maintain secrecy, to activate the pool too late and said given the option, he would always lean toward secrecy if it meant protecting the troops.[97]

THE PERSIAN GULF WAR

Although secrecy was ostensibly the reason for restricting press access to Grenada and Panama, there was little doubt that the United States was going to war against Iraq over its invasion of neighboring Kuwait. The buildup to war was relatively lengthy, with President George H. W. Bush first telling Iraq's leader Saddam Hussein to leave Kuwait, then starting a massive military buildup in the Gulf region. The war was seen as so inevitable that a CNN crew set up shop in a Baghdad hotel and reported live when U.S. planes began bombing Iraq. For the first time, the American public could watch on live television as a war started.

Once the war began, it became apparent that media coverage of war had entered new territory. With the development of satellite communications, much of what was happening could be reported live on television in the United States—and presumably anyone could view it, including the Iraqi government, which had access to satellite reception. The live aspect of the war was enhanced by the development of 24-hour cable news, creating an insatiable need for more and more "new" news. This live war coverage created a problem for reporters attending military briefings in the war zone. It is common practice for journalists, in an effort to find out as much as they can, to ask questions that they suspect will not be answered. During the live briefings, the journalists asked repeated questions about tactics or troop movements that the military officers who were conducting the briefings would not answer. The questions and refusals to answer became so ingrained in the public's consciousness that a Saturday Night Live comedy skit during the war was based on reporters asking inane questions such as "where exactly are our troops located."

One reporter who came in for particular criticism was CNN correspondent Peter Arnett, a reporter who won the Pulitzer Prize for his reporting from Vietnam and who had often angered those in the Pentagon and elsewhere in government because of his unflattering stories. Arnett had been one of the CNN employees who broadcast the start of the war live from a Baghdad hotel, and after the ground war began he reported from Iraqi territory. His reporting was subject to Iraqi censorship, which CNN noted whenever it aired his reports. When Arnett reported that U.S. bombs were hitting civilian targets, 21 members of the House of Representatives signed a letter asking CNN to stop broadcasting his reports because they were discouraging troops and the American public. Senator Alan Simpson of Wyoming called Arnett a "sympathizer" and criticized his reporting from Vietnam two decades earlier, accusing Arnett of having a Vietnamese brother-in-law who worked with the Vietcong. Simpson later apologized for his incorrect statements about Arnett's Vietnamese relationships.[98]

The Pentagon began making plans to activate the press pool even before the war started. Pool journalists would be subject to review by military censors. In addition, the pool reporters would be accompanied at all times by military press officers, prompting complaints by journalists that the military personnel whom they would be interviewing would be inhibited from voicing unpopular opinions by the presence of an officer who would be recording everything the personnel said.

Gary Woodward, in the book *Media and the Persian Gulf War,* writes that the pool system worked well sometimes: "Some escorts were helpful in getting reporters to key locations and helping them see particular aspects of military operations, especially in its early phases. But more aggressive members of the press viewed the system as an effective filter that worked against the press and in favor of the ostensible news management objectives of the military."[99] The system was designed not to encourage reporting but to limit what journalists saw and what they could report. Some escorts went so far as to tell soldiers not to answer some questions, and when reporters started interviewing soldiers at a restaurant without a supervising officer present, the supervising officer said he would send someone to a fast-food restaurant in Dhahran to make sure no one talked to journalists unless someone from the military press office was present. In another incident, a military escort who objected to an analysis written by a reporter from the British *Independent* tried to have that reporter removed from a pool.[100] Some reports were delayed by censorship so long that the news became outdated before it was ever cleared. Other stories were either altered—describing returning bomber pilots as "proud" rather than "giddy"—or killed outright, such as stories that said Christian church services were held for Marines in Muslim Saudi Arabia or that pilots relaxed between flights by watching sexually explicit movies. Other stories were "lost" when censors objected to a journalist's previous reporting.[101]

Some reporters felt so encumbered by the press pool system that they went "unilateral," entering the war zone on their own, without military escorts, risking arrest and eviction from the war zone by U.S. forces, or seizure and possible imprisonment by Iraqi forces. A CBS crew headed by correspondent Bob Simon, for instance, disappeared while on a unilateral reporting excursion; it turned out they had been arrested by Iraqi soldiers.[102]

As the ground war began, the military began a new method of ensuring positive coverage, using military aircraft to fly in hundreds of local newspaper and television reporters from smaller cities around the country. These reporters would stay in the area for a few days, preparing reports about hometown soldiers, and then be flown back to the United States, to be replaced by more local journalists. Positive news was the Pentagon's goal. One of the enduring images of the Vietnam War showed dozens of flag-draped caskets carrying dead soldiers as they were unloaded from cargo planes and lined up on the tarmac. The White House was intent on not repeating that; therefore, the air force refused to allow journalists to have access to Dover Air Force Base to photograph or film the flag-draped caskets of the Persian Gulf War dead. News media attempts to win a court order permitting them access to the base failed when a U.S. district court judge ruled that the military was acting within its power to control access to a military base.

SOMALIA, HAITI, AND BOSNIA

The end of the Persian Gulf War brought a number of critiques by journalists and academic writers examining how the military–press relationship had deteriorated and making recommendations for the future. When 30,000 U.S. troopers traveled to Somalia in 1992 to protect the distribution of food and other aid, the media did not wait for the military to tell them when and where to report. Instead, they traveled on their own to Somalia and reported where they wanted. In Haiti, where U.S. Marines waded ashore to aid in humanitarian efforts in 1994, the media were already there; one of the enduring images of that event is of television cameras, lights blazing, filming the marines as they came ashore in full battle gear.[103] But it was in Haiti that the first embedding of reporters began. For the first time, reporters were allowed to "embed" themselves within a particular military unit, going where the soldiers went and observing the action firsthand.

Embedding became more common in 1996 when the United States entered Bosnia to quell racial cleansing that was occurring in the Balkan country. This was the first time the term *embedding* became part of the military–press vernacular, as 33 journalists were embedded in 15 military units.[104] The Pentagon had strict rules for these embedded reporters, however. If the reporters were embedded for more than 24 hours, they had to get permission to quote the soldiers they were with, and everything they saw was considered to be off-the-record background information.[105]

Embedding was again employed in 1999 when NATO, including the United States, began bombing Kosovo because of the Milosevic government's ethnic cleansing policies; because the conflict was primarily air-based, media members had little opportunity to accompany the military units. Therefore, many journalists reported from Kosovo, getting much of their information from the Milosevic government, occasionally reporting stories such as the mistaken bombing of a refugee camp and reporting Milosevic's defense that no ethnic cleansing was occurring.[106] The air war over Kosovo and journalists' efforts to bypass military control of their reporting caused renewed hostility between the two sides. War historian Douglas Porch writes that the media "inevitably, then, was wary of information supplied by the military. Press conferences evoked the media's unhappy Gulf War memories of press pools, denial of access, obfuscation, and apparent manipulation; the press resolved not to be fooled twice. Because [the press] had scant access to Kosovo, it could not see 'ethnic cleansing.' Nor could it effectively cover the air war."[107]

TERRORISM AND THE WARS IN AFGHANISTAN AND IRAQ

The terrorist attacks on New York, Washington, D.C., and Flight 93, which crashed in Pennsylvania, on September 11, 2001, in what became known as 9/11, marked the beginning of two wars and two distinct ways of reporting war. President George W. Bush almost immediately announced that the United States was at war with terrorists, stating during a speech before Congress on September 20 that "either you are with us or you are with the terrorists."[108] The first effort to root out support of terrorism was to attack Al Qaeda (the terrorist organization that orchestrated the attacks), its training camps, and the ruling Taliban, all in Afghanistan.

The war in Afghanistan, while no surprise to anyone in the United States or Afghanistan, was still waged in relative secrecy. Much of the early fighting involved special forces troops operating deep within Afghanistan, and operational secrecy meant that no reporters were allowed to cover these incursions. As in Kosovo, some journalists made their way to Kabul, the capital of Afghanistan, to report on their own. In addition, the Qatari-based satellite television network Al-Jazeera broadcast from an Arab perspective, although its critics—including many in the U.S. government—said it was biased against America. Al-Jazeera officials said it was no accident that their Kabul office was hit by a U.S. bomb on November 3, 2001.[109]

As the war in Afghanistan continued, the Bush administration began making plans to attack Iraq, ostensibly because Saddam Hussein might have weapons of mass destruction—fears that turned out to be unfounded. As the Department of Defense began planning for the war, officials recognized the need to arrange for press coverage of a war that would dwarf the size of the conflicts in either Kosovo or Afghanistan, taking into account intense media interest in an Iraq War while at the same time maintaining control over the message in an era of immediate communication. The solution was a greatly expanded system of embedding. In January 2002, representatives of the major media outlets met with Department of Defense officials to plan how the press would cover the incipient war.

The Department of Defense decided that a huge embedded-reporter program would serve two purposes. It would give the press access to the battlefield, and, through their reporting, particularly television broadcasts, it would intimidate the Iraqis, who could watch as the overwhelming U.S. forces streamed into their country. More than 700 journalists were embedded during the opening days of the Iraq War, including 400 with army units.[110] Embedded journalists had ground rules—for instance, they could not report the location of troops nor the identity of the killed or wounded—but they were free to report what they witnessed. In one high-profile incident, Fox News correspondent Geraldo Rivera was ordered out of Iraq after he violated the rules by drawing the location of his unit in the sand with a stick while on camera.

Written criticism of the embedded-reporter policy fell into two categories. First, journalists reporting from an embedded unit saw the war only from that unit's perspective. A reporter traveling in an armored personnel vehicle cannot be expected to see the big picture. Second, journalists whose very life depends on the soldiers in the unit where they are embedded would naturally be reluctant to report wrongdoing, mistakes, or even crimes committed by those soldiers. Media critic Andrew Hoskins casts this second criticism as replacing "the standard fare of pool and recorded reports compiled from news agencies" with "hundreds of truly unique perspectives."[111]

As troops entered Baghdad, ending the early part of the war, most of the embedded reporters gave up their spots to report from the capital city on their own or "went unilateral," to use a phrase popularized in the Persian Gulf War.

CONCLUSION

The aims of the military, with its goals of protecting information, maintaining the element of surprise, and controlling the public's perception of military and government leaders, have long been in conflict with the aims of the press, with its goals of learning information and reporting that information to the public. Whether under General Sherman during the Civil War, General MacArthur during the Korean War, or the Department of Defense during the War on Terror, efforts to control the media, and therefore the message, have long been at the heart of censorship during wartime.

Douglas Porch puts the conflict this way: "The basic nature and goals of the two institutions [military and press] are fundamentally in tension. For its part, the military, like most bureaucracies, prefers to do its business behind closed doors.... The press, however, responds to the requirement of democracy to expose the actions of government—including, especially, the military—to public scrutiny."[112] At the same time, the military and the press have a common goal: serving the public.[113] The differences, however, usually outweigh that common goal.

In addition, military policy, especially in the twenty-first century, is more often made by political leaders, whose goal is not only military victory but also victory in the area of public opinion. At times, censorship decisions have been based less on military objectives and more on political purposes. The saying that "truth is the first casualty of war" takes on added meaning when the truth is replaced by propaganda.

As the United States moves forward in the twenty-first century, it seems certain there will continue to be wars. How the White House, Pentagon, and military officers in the field deal with the question of media coverage, particularly in an era in which anyone with a cell phone camera or a laptop computer and an Internet connection can become a journalist, will determine whether the public will get an unvarnished view of war or a sanitized version whose main purpose is to keep the government happy.

NOTES

1. Nathaniel Lande, *Dispatches from the Front: News Accounts of American Wars, 1776–1991* (New York: Henry Holt, 1995), 8–11.

2. Lloyd J. Matthews, "Preface," in *Newsmen and National Defense: Is Conflict Inevitable?* ed. Lloyd J. Matthews (Washington: Brassley's, 1991), ix–xii, esp. ix.

3. Donna Lee Dickerson, *The Course of Tolerance: Freedom of the Press in Nineteenth Century America* (New York: Greenwood Press, 1990), 40–42.

4. Ibid., 39.

5. Ibid., 46.

6. Lande, *Dispatches from the Front,* 45.

7. Dickerson, *Course of Tolerance,* 47–48.

8. Lande, *Dispatches from the Front,* 49–51.

9. Ibid., 90–91.

10. The Associated Press (AP) is credited with developing the notion of neutral, objective reporting. Before the AP, the nation's newspapers were largely partisan, with most stories taking an editorial stance and expressing the writer's or the editor's opinions. But the AP was designed to provide news to newspapers of all political persuasions, so that its stories had to be acceptable to all, that is, neutral and not partisan.

11. Dickerson, *Course of Tolerance,* 144.

12. Ibid., 145.

13. Joseph H. Ewing, "The New Sherman Letters," in Matthews, *Newsmen and National Defense,* 19–29, esp. 19.

14. Christopher Andrew, *For the President's Eyes Only: Secret Intelligence and the American Presidency from Washington to Bush* (New York: HarperCollins, 1995), 14.

15. Stanley P. Hirschon, *The White Tecumseh: A Biography of William T. Sherman* (New York: John Wiley and Sons, 1997), 96.

16. Ibid., 100–101.

17. Ewing, "New Sherman Letters," 22.

18. Lande, *Dispatches from the Front,* 110.

19. Ibid., 111–12.

20. Hirschon, *White Tecumseh,* 146–49.

21. Dickerson, *Course of Tolerance,* 147.

22. Ibid., 148–50.

23. Dickerson, *Course of Tolerance,* 154–55.

24. Ibid., 156–57.

25. Geoffrey R. Stone, *War and Liberty: An American Dilemma:1790 to the Present* (New York: W. W. Norton, 2007), 38.

26. Dickerson, *Course of Tolerance,* 167.

27. Ibid., 170–71.

28. Brayton Harris, *Blue and Gray in Black and White: Newspapers in the Civil War* (Washington, DC: Bratsford Brassey, 1999), 103–4.

29. Dickerson, *Course of Tolerance,* 155.

30. Ibid., 169.

31. Harris, *Blue and Gray,* 106.

32. Donald E. Reynolds, *Editors Make War: Southern Newspapers in the Secession Crisis* (Nashville, TN: Vanderbilt University Press, 1970), 174.

33. Harris, *Blue and Gray,* 109–13.

34. Dickerson, *Course of Tolerance,* 232–33.

35. William M. Hammond, "The Army and Public Affairs: A Glance Back," in Matthews, *Newsmen and National Defense,* 1–16, esp. 6.

36. Dickerson, *Course of Tolerance,* 234–35.

37. Ibid., 235.

38. Smith, Jeffrey A. *War and Press Freedom: The Problem of Prerogative Power* (New York: Oxford University Press, 1999), 122.

39. Ibid., 236.

40. Randall S. Sumpter, "'Censorship Liberally Administered': Press, U.S. Military Relations in the Spanish-American War," *Communication Law and Policy* 4, no. 4 (Autumn 1999): 463–81, esp. 469.

41. Smith, *War and Press Freedom,* 123.

42. Sumpter, "'Censorship Liberally Administered,'" 480.

43. Dickerson, *Course of Tolerance,* 235.

44. Stone, *War and Liberty,* 46–48.

45. Smith, *War and Press Freedom,* 129.

46. James R. Mock, *Censorship 1917* (Princeton, NJ: Princeton University Press, 1941), 39.

47. Stone, *War and Liberty,* 49–50.

48. Mock, *Censorship 1917,* 48.

49. Stone, *War and Liberty,* 130.

50. Mock, *Censorship 1917,* 52.

51. Ibid., 148.

52. Hammond, "Army and Public Affairs," 7.

53. Smith, *War and Press Freedom,* 140–41.

54. Ibid., 142.

55. Mock, *Censorship 1917,* 176.

56. Hammond, "Army and Public Affairs," 8.

57. Mock, *Censorship 1917,* 94–95.

58. Smith, *War and Press Freedom,* 158–59.

59. Robert Henson, "The Muzzling of World War II Radio Weathercasts," *Weatherwise* 56, no. 3 (May–June 2003): 20–21.

60. Michael S. Sweeney, *Secrets of Victory: The Office of Censorship and the American Press and Radio in World War II* (Chapel Hill: University of North Carolina Press, 2001), 100–101.

61. Ibid., 7.

62. Michael S. Sweeney, "Censorship Missionaries of World War II," *Journalism History* 27 (2001): 4–13.

63. Robert W. Desmond, *Tides of War: World News Reporting 1940–1945* (Iowa City: University of Iowa Press, 1984), 224.

64. Smith, *War and Press Freedom,* 152.

65. Ibid., 146.

66. Sweeney, *Secrets of Victory,* 92–96.

67. Desmond, *Tides of War,* 221–22.

68. Edwin Emery, *The Press and America: An Interpretive History of the Mass Media* (Englewood Cliffs, NJ: Prentice-Hall, 1972), 528.

69. Walter Cronkite, *A Reporter's Life* (New York: Alfred A. Knopf, 1996), 98.

70. Ibid., 99.

71. Douglas Porch, "'No Bad Stories': The American Media-Military Relationship," *Naval War College Review* 55, no. 1 (2002): 85–107, esp. 88.

72. Dan Rather, "Truth on the Battlefield," *Harvard International Review* 23, no.1 (Spring 2001): 66–71, esp. 67.

73. Smith, *War and Press Freedom,* 164–65.

74. Ibid., 166–67.

75. Ibid., 168.

76. Ibid., 169–71.

77. James Aronson, *The Press and the Cold War* (New York: Bobbs Merrill, 1970), 114–15.

78. Ibid., 115.

79. Hammond, "Army and Public Affairs," 12.

80. Aronson, *Press and the Cold War,* 107.

81. Ibid., 127–52.

82. Daniel C. Hallin, *The 'Uncensored War': The Media and Vietnam* (New York: Oxford University Press, 1986), 6.

83. Ibid., 39.

84. Smith, *War and Press Freedom,* 181–82.

85. Hallin, *'Uncensored War,'* 129.

86. Peter Braestrup, "Censored," *New Republic* 204, no. 6 (1991): 16–17.

87. Hallin, *'Uncensored War,'* 130.

88. Braestrup, "Censored," 16.

89. Andrew J. Huebner, "Rethinking American Press Coverage of the Vietnam War, 1965–68," *Journalism History* 31, no. 3 (2005): 150–61, esp. 151.

90. Bruce Cumings, *War and Television* (London: Verso, 1992), 88.

91. Hallin, *'Uncensored War,'* 177.

92. Hammond, "Army and Public Affairs," 14.

93. Smith, *War and Press Freedom,* 189.

94. Ibid.

95. Barry E. Willey, "Military-Media Relations Come of Age," in Matthews, *Newsmen and National Defense,* 81–89.

96. Jacqueline Sharkey, *Under Fire: U.S. Military Restrictions on the Media from Grenada to the Persian Gulf* (Washington, DC: Center for Public Integrity, 1991), 72–80.

97. Fred S. Hoffman, "The Panama Press Pool Deployment: A Critique," in Matthews, *Newsmen and National Defense,* 91–109.

98. Sharkey, *Under Fire,* 141–42.

99. Gary C. Woodward, "The Rules of the Game: The Military and the Press in the Persian Gulf War," in *The Media and the Persian Gulf War,* ed. Robert E. Denton Jr. (Westport, CT: Praeger, 1993), 1–26, esp. 15.

100. Sharkey, *Under Fire,* 134.

101. Woodward, "Rules of the Game," 16.

102. Sharkey, *Under Fire,* 129–30.

103. Christopher Paul and James J. Kim, *Reporters on the Battlefield: The Embedded Press in Historical Context* (Arlington, VA: Rand Corporation, 2004), 46, 73.

104. Ibid., 48.

105. Smith, *War and Press Freedom,* 46–47.

106. Paul and Kim, *Reporters on the Battlefield,* 46.

107. Porch, "'No Bad Stories,'" 99.

108. George W. Bush, "Address to a Joint Session of Congress and the American People." United States Capitol, Washington, D.C., September 20, 2001. Available at http://www.whitehouse.gov/news/releases/2001/09/20010920-8.html.

109. David Dadge, *Casualty of War: The Bush Administration's Assault on a Free Press* (Amherst: Prometheus Books, 2004), 66.

110. Paul and Kim, *Reporters on the Battlefield,* 53–54.

111. Andrew Hoskins, *Televising War from Vietnam to Iraq* (London: Continuum, 2004), 127.

112. Porch, "'No Bad Stories,'" 86.

113. Paul and Kim, *Reporters on the Battlefield,* xiv.

3

Censorship of Books

The public school system in Kanawha County, West Virginia, erupted in an explosion of violence in 1974. What began as a simple protest over the county board of education's selection of textbooks turned violent as summer turned into fall. Classes and businesses were boycotted. Coal miners walked off the job. School buses were hit by gunfire. Elementary schools were firebombed. The board of education office was dynamited.

What became known as the Kanawha textbook controversy began on April 11, 1974, when the five-member Kanawha County Board of Education voted after lengthy debate to adopt a series of 330 language arts textbooks.[1] Critics alleged that the books promoted anti-Christian values such as stealing and lying, used profanity and other improper language, and ignored "traditional American values." L. W. Seaman, president of the Kanawha County Parent-Teacher Association (PTA) Council, said the disputed texts were "woefully lacking in morally uplifting ideas."[2] Among the most commonly cited complaints were examples such as third-grade texts suggesting that teachers have their students compare the stories of "Androcles and the Lion" and "Daniel in the Lion's Den" (which protesters said compares a fable with a biblical, and therefore true, account), and the Mark Twain story "Adam's Diary," which (in the protesters' view) gave a sacrilegious account of how Adam named all things in the new garden of Eden.[3] As the protest continued, various factions chimed in with their own objections, calling for the removal of works by authors such as Kurt Vonnegut, James Fennimore Cooper, Washington Irving, and Ernest Hemingway.[4] The board of education, finally meeting to act on the purchase of the books it had adopted in April, voted in June to buy all but eight of the textbook titles.[5]

The textbook protest, which had been simmering for months, erupted when the fall semester began. During the first week of classes, enrollment was down 20 percent as parents boycotted schools to voice their protest over the textbooks. To make an impact, parents picketed the region's numerous heavily unionized coal mines, and 6,000 miners stayed off the job rather than cross picket lines; likewise, several construction sites were shut down by picketing parents. Kanawha County's public bus system was idled when drivers joined the boycott, leaving 11,000 riders without transportation.[6] U.S. marshals were ordered into the area to enforce an order by U.S. District Judge Dennis Knapp prohibiting textbook protesters from picketing businesses— an order that was roundly ignored.[7] Like a virus, the dispute spread, idling schools and businesses in adjacent counties that were not directly involved in the textbook protest.

The textbook protest soon turned violent. The Reverend Charles Quigley, one of the protest leaders, announced he was praying for God to strike dead the school board members who had voted for the texts.[8] Several schools were rocked by bombs, shots were fired at school buses, and a dynamite blast hit the school board office, just a block from the state capitol. In the face of mounting lawlessness, the school board voted to give parents veto power over the textbooks used for their children.[9] Sporadic violence continued for several months, however. In one of the more bizarre episodes of the aftermath, four of the five county school board members and county School Superintendent Kenneth Underwood were arrested at the request of a textbook protester who persuaded a county magistrate to charge them with contributing to the delinquency of a minor—charges that were later dropped.[10] A number of private, church-related schools sprang up in Kanawha County, and the exodus of those students whose parents were most vocal in their textbook opposition helped bring a gradual calm to the county's public schools.[11] In the ensuing months, federal prosecutors won convictions of nine textbook protesters in the school bombings. By fall 1975, the textbook protest was essentially over, and calm returned. During the protest, an estimated 20 percent of the county's public school students missed at least two months of classes, and in some parts of the county the figure was closer to 50 percent.[12]

EARLY CENSORSHIP

The violent and divisive dispute over school texts in Kanawha County might be easily dismissed as an isolated incident, if American history were not filled with examples of book banning. Prosecution of writers, publishers, and sellers of books dates to the early days of this country. Peter Holmes was convicted in 1821 of publishing an obscene book, John Cleland's *Memoirs of a Woman of Pleasure* (although the same book was declared not obscene by the U.S. Supreme Court in 1963).[13] Walt Whitman's classic book of poetry, *Leaves of Grass,* was declared obscene as soon as it was published in 1855, and Whitman lost his job in the U.S. Department of the Interior 10 years later when his boss found a copy of the book in Whitman's desk drawer.[14] As recounted in more detail in chapter 5, antipornography crusader Anthony Comstock succeeded in having Congress ban (through the aptly named Comstock Act) the mailing of obscene material, including books. Jean-Jacques Rousseau's 1884 book *Confessions* was banned from importation into the United States by customs officials in 1929 as "injurious to public morals" because of its sexual content.[15] Thomas Hardy's classic *Jude the Obscure* had to be edited and the title changed to *Hearts Insurgent* before it could be published in America in 1895; as an example of the edits, the two children in the book who are born out of wedlock to Jude and Sue became orphans adopted by the couple.[16]

The James Joyce novel *Ulysses* (1918) was the subject of repeated censorship and eventually a landmark court ruling. Written in a stream-of-consciousness style, told from the points of view of three people on one day, the book includes some sexual references. It encountered problems immediately upon arrival in the United States. The post office burned 500 copies, and in 1932, when it was shipped to this country, it was declared obscene by the customs office. The publisher, Random House, filed a lawsuit in federal court asking that the book be cleared for distribution.[17] In *United States v. One Book Called "Ulysses,"* the U.S. Second Circuit Court of Appeals ruled that a book could not be labeled as obscene based on isolated sections of the work; rather, the book had to be judged on its entirety.[18]

Political as well as sexual content could lead to criminal prosecution for mere possession of a book. Hinton Helper's 1859 antislavery book, *The Impending Crisis in the South—How to Meet It,* was roundly criticized in the South, and arrests occurred in Maryland, Virginia, North Carolina, and South Carolina for possession of Helper's book; in Arkansas three men were hanged for having the book in their possession.[19]

EARLY TWENTIETH-CENTURY BOOKS

Book censorship also occurred during World War I, as both government agencies and watchful citizens kept a close eye on what Americans read. For instance, Sigmund Freud's book *Reflections on War and Death* came to the attention of chief government censor George Creel because it contained a passage on page 14 stating that in times of war, a nation is free to use injustice, violence, and lies to achieve its goals.[20] Creel also complained about other books that he thought favored America's enemy in the war, Germany, and he referred one book, *The Imprisoned Freeman,* to the Federal Bureau of Investigation because he thought it was German propaganda and should be banned. The post office banned the mailing of "anti-American" books, and H. G. Wells's 1908 book *The War in the Air,* in which he envisioned air attacks on the United States by Germany, was banned from the mail because it was not the kind of book that would instill confidence in U.S. efforts in Europe. The head of the Library of Congress, Dr. Herbert Putnam, cooperated with the War Department in suppressing harmful books that were destined for military camps. Similarly, the army itself banned from its libraries books that described the horrors of war in general or that were viewed as favorable toward Germany.[21]

Ironically, a number of books written in the early years of the United States faced censorship not when they were first written but decades or even a century later. Nathaniel Hawthorne's *The Scarlet Letter,* written in 1850, was removed from an English classroom in Michigan in 1977 and struck from the recommended reading list because of objections by a school principal and a parent who objected to the theme of adultery.[22] Mark Twain's 1885 book *Huckleberry Finn* is one of the most censored books in America, at first because it was considered to be a bad influence on young readers and later because of its frequent use of the word *nigger.* It was thrown out of the Denver Library in 1902, and by 1907 it had been removed from libraries across the country. The New York Board of Education, at the urging of the National Association for the Advancement of Colored People (NAACP), removed it from school libraries because of its "racially offensive" language. Ironically, it was also removed from the Mark Twain Intermediate School in Fairfax County, Virginia, in 1982.[23] It continues to be one of the most challenged books in libraries across the country, and some teachers are reluctant even to assign *Huckleberry Finn* or another Twain book, *The Adventures of Tom Sawyer,* because of the history of conflict and opposition.[24]

CENSORSHIP INCREASES

Although censorship of books has occurred throughout U.S. history, a confluence of three developments led to a tremendous increase in book censorship beginning in the 1940s. First, reaction to Communist advances in Europe, particularly in Russia in the years after World War I, led to an effort by some in government to uncover Communists or Communist sympathizers, best illustrated by Senator Joseph McCarthy's campaign (in what became known as McCarthyism) and the House Un-American Activities Committee, which attempted to ferret out sedition in government and the entertainment field. Second, at the same time this red scare was in full force, English departments around the country began to move away from teaching literature using the classics and to use more modern writers, some of whom were tackling controversial topics such as sex, racism, and capitalism. Third, the number of school libraries and the number of books they held began to explode.[25]

The 1940s saw books not only censored but also burned, because they were seen as supporting Communism or opposing U.S. efforts in World War II. Book burning has a long history in America, beginning in 1650 when *The Meritorious Price of Our Redemption,* by William Pynchon, was set aflame in Boston's marketplace because its religious point of view differed from that of the colony.[26] In 1743, a bonfire in New London, in what later became Connecticut, burned books that were considered frivolous or subversive to religion.[27] As mentioned earlier, 500 copies of *Ulysses* were burned by the post office in 1922, and New York City police burned hundreds of books in 1935 and 1936. In addition, three copies of the John Steinbeck novel *Grapes of Wrath* were burned in St. Louis in 1939.[28]

Even so, burning and other forms of destruction reached their zenith in the 1940s and 1950s. Post office officials seized and destroyed 600 tons of foreign-published books between December 1940 and December 1941.[29] In Sapulpa, Oklahoma, several books were burned in the early 1950s as being unsuitable for children to read.[30]

LIBRARIES AND SCHOOLS

Book burning experienced a resurgence in the 1970s and 1980s as parents, upset with the reading material their children were being given in the public schools, took matters into their own hands. Organized book burnings took place in Seminole, Oklahoma, Alliance, Nebraska, Warsaw, Indiana, Morgantown, West Virginia, and other cities. Among the books that were burned were *The Hobbit* by J.R.R. Tolkien and some Harlequin romance novels.[31] Thirty-four copies of Kurt Vonnegut's *Slaughterhouse-Five* were burned in Drake, North Dakota, in 1973.[32]

The red scare and the anti-Communist movements led to official censorship, as well as self-censorship by authors, librarians, and publishers. Book publishers, for example, were urged to remain vigilant against books that might be objectionable. Bennett Cerf, president of Random House and Modern Library book publishers, urged his colleagues to engage in self-censorship to avoid official governmental action, telling them in a magazine article to avoid "sly or poisonous propaganda" and recommending that they perform "a service to [their] country by deliberately sabotaging" such books.[33]

Steinbeck's *The Grapes of Wrath,* which tells the story of the Joad family, who were forced to move from their home in Oklahoma to a new life in California because of the Depression and the Dust Bowl in the Midwest, was banned almost as soon as it was published in 1939. In Kansas City, Missouri, the board of education banned it from public libraries, and it was likewise taken off the shelves in Kern County, California (although later restocked), Greene County, Ohio, and even the library aboard the USS *Tennessee.* What caused the uproar was both Steinbeck's language and his descriptions of the poor who were afflicted by circumstances outside of their control, or what censors said was the implication that the poor were ignorant and filthy and did not take advantage of numerous social service agencies.[34]

Librarians, set upon by censors such as those in the Steinbeck case, took action, with the American Library Association (ALA) adopting the Library Bill of Rights in 1939, establishing that libraries should select books "because of interest and value to the people of the community, and in no case should selection be influenced by the race or nationality or the political or religious views of the writers."[35] The Library Bill of Rights was amended in 1969, and the ALA further amended it in 1986, suggesting that school libraries should support free and open access to information.[36] Of course, that did not stop censorship attempts, particularly with books many today consider classics.

CENSORSHIP OF CLASSIC BOOKS

Ray Bradbury's *Fahrenheit 451,* which, ironically, deals with the issue of book burning, was printed in 1953, and in 1967 the publisher, Ballantine Books, distributed a heavily edited version that deleted words such as *hell, damn,* and *abortion* so that it could be sold to high schools. It was 13 years before Bradbury learned of the bowdlerized[37] version of his book about censorship. Ballantine then agreed to his demand that it stop selling the cleaned-up version.[38]

Lady Chatterley's Lover by D. H. Lawrence, originally published in Italy in 1928 and later in the United States as well, contains frank sexual material in the story of a disabled husband whose wife has an affair with the gardener. An attempt by a New York bookseller, James A. Delacey, to buy five copies of the book resulted in his arrest, along with the arrest of his clerk; both were convicted of selling an obscene book, and Delacey was sentenced to four months in jail. The book was subject to seizure for obscenity through the 1950s, and it was not until 1959 that a U.S. district judge in *Grove Press v. Christenberry*[39] ruled that the post office could not ban it from the mail.[40]

Another classic book, *Lolita* by Vladimir Nabokov, about a man's sexual infatuation with a 12-year-old girl, has predictably encountered censorship.

Nabokov had trouble finding a publisher in the United States, with several declining the book because they feared trouble. Once he found a publisher, the book did encounter censorship, as the Cincinnati, Ohio, public library, for instance, banned the book from its shelves.[41]

The publisher who finally printed Lawrence's book, Barney Rosset of Grove Press, published several other controversial books, including *Memoirs of a Woman of Pleasure* (which led to the Supreme Court decision concerning obscenity), Henry Miller's *Tropic of Cancer,* and *Naked Lunch* by William Burroughs. Rosset was in and out of court for the books he published as officials tried to prevent distribution of the books, regarding them as an affront to public morals.[42]

SCHOOL BOARDS AND BOOKS

Some of the most vigorous fights over books have involved the selection of textbooks, with advocates from both the Right and Left attempting to persuade publishers to produce schoolbooks that reflect their view of how society ought to be. During the 1960s and 1970s, in communities large and small, parents and school board members took steps to limit what books were available to their children both in school libraries and on approved classroom reading lists. One of the major battlefields in this fight was Chelsea, Massachusetts, where the father of a 14-year-old complained to the mayor in 1977 about a poem in a book his daughter borrowed from a school library. The poem, written by a 15-year-old who won a contest and had her poem published in an anthology, is graphic in its sexuality. It tells of "one million horny lip-smacking men" who are "All begging for a lay, a little pussy, a little tit...." A campaign led by the publisher of the local newspaper, Andrew Quigley, called the poem "dirty rotten filth," whereas the local school board voted to leave the anthology on the library shelves, but only if the page containing the poem, "The City to a Young Girl," was ripped out.

The Massachusetts Library Association and another group, the Right to Read Defense Committee, filed suit in U.S. district court seeking to prevent the school board from carrying out its plan. A year later, Judge Joseph Tauro ruled that the book could stay on the shelves without alteration. He wrote in his decision that although a school board can determine what books will be purchased for a library, the same school officials might not have the authority to remove a book that they later find objectionable. Meanwhile, the school board first voted unanimously to fire the librarian, then later to retain her, under threat of another lawsuit.[43]

Tauro's decision presented a problem: how much power do school officials have to remove a book from a library? The U.S. Supreme Court answered that question to some degree. In *Island Trees Union Free School District v. Pico,*[44] the Supreme Court was asked to determine whether a New York State public school district was within its rights to remove nine books from the school library. Among the books removed were *Slaughterhouse-Five* by Kurt Vonnegut, *Best Short Stories by Negro Writers,* and *Black Boy* by Richard Wright. Five students sued the school board, seeking an injunction to keep the books in the library. The students lost at trial when the judge deferred to local control of the schools. When the court of appeals voted 2–1 to send the case back to the district court for a retrial, the school board asked the Supreme Court to step in.

The Court's decision said that local school boards have broad discretion in the management of schools, but also that local school officials have to abide by the First Amendment. The Court ruled that a school library is a place where students can go to be exposed to new ideas:

If a Democratic school board, motivated by party affiliation, ordered the removal of all books written by or in favor of Republicans, few would doubt that the order violated the constitutional rights of the students denied access to those books. The same conclusion would surely apply if an all-white school board, motivated by racial animus, decided to remove all books authored by blacks or advocating racial equality and integration. Our Constitution does not permit the official suppression of ideas. Thus, whether petitioners' removal of books from their school libraries denied respondents their First Amendment rights depends upon the motivation behind petitioners' actions. If petitioners intended by their removal decision to deny respondents access to ideas with which petitioners disagreed, and if this intent was the decisive factor in petitioners' decision, then petitioners have exercised their discretion in violation of the Constitution.[45]

Richard Peltz, writing in the *Brigham Young University Education and Law Journal,* argues that rather than making a clear ruling, in *Pico* the Court further muddied the waters regarding censorship in libraries. The decision concerned not the usual public library with which Americans interact routinely but a high school library. Further clouding the outcome was the fact that although a majority of the Court ruled that censorship was unconstitutional, there was no majority agreement as to why, reducing the decision's value as legal precedent. In addition to the ruling, two concurring opinions and four dissenting opinions were written. In fact, despite the *Pico* decision, censorship in the schools continued.

RELIGIOUS OBJECTIONS TO BOOKS

Texas was the scene for some of these textbook fights in the 1970s and 1980s, when Mel and Norma Gabler from Longview, Texas, opposed what they considered to be inappropriate textbooks. And textbook selection in Texas was important; the state spent $60 million a year on textbooks for public schools, and textbook publishers believed they needed to produce books suitable to that large market; therefore, what was acceptable in Texas was the standard for the rest of the country.[46] The Gablers argued that textbooks should be edited line by line to remove anything that did not promote American values or conform to the Gablers' conservative Christian religious beliefs. In just one instance, they provided 659 pages of items they objected to in literature and American history texts.[47]

The Gablers' mission caught the attention of several groups, including Phyllis Schlafly and her Eagle Forum, which formed the ironically named Stop Textbook Censorship Committee, targeting what it said were attempts by liberals to eliminate religious material from texts. "The list is endless of the topics and the books which the liberals have censored out of the school curriculum, out of schools and the libraries and the media," Schlafly wrote, citing creationism, prayer, and references to God.[48]

The fight over textbooks in Texas was revived in 1994, when the board of education was debating the selection of health textbooks. Among deletions the Texas Board of Education required were the entries on breast or prostate cancer self-examination (it might lead to self-stimulation), as well as limitations on the discussion of homosexuality.

The list of books struck from school reading lists and school libraries is too long to recount in this book, but some of the works that have been censored include *A Farewell to Arms* by Ernest Hemingway, *Catcher in the Rye* by J. D. Salinger, *A Clockwork Orange* by Anthony Burgess, *Catch-22* by Joseph Heller, and *1984* by George Orwell.

One opponent of the way schools select books is Washington, D.C., educator Onalee McGraw, who argues in her book *Secular Humanism and the Schools* that the public schools have been promoting an anti-God curriculum that advocates secular humanism, which she and others equate with a competing religious message. Secular humanism, she argues, promotes permissiveness in society and replaces the absolutes of Christianity with moral relativism.[49] Secular humanism being taught in the schools as an alternative, government-sanctioned religious viewpoint is a common complaint of some conservative Christian parents. Matthew Moen, writing in the *NEA Higher Education Journal,* states the quandary thus: " 'Which is the greater evil,' they ask rhetorically, 'to take books off the shelves (that contain sexual imagery), or to put books in that cast the Pilgrims as happy adventurers rather than religious believers escaping persecution?' "[50]

In her book about the conservative Christian movement, *Not by Politics Alone,* Sara Diamond writes that those who want to restrict access to books in the schools are trying to prevent the moral values of their homes from being usurped by so-called government schools: "Under the banner of family values, innumerable battles have been fought over materials available to children in public schools and libraries. Critics charge 'censorship,' and yet members of the Christian Right claim that all they want is to protect young minds."[51]

COURT CASES SINCE *PICO*

In the years since the *Pico* case, parents have tried going to court to force school officials to remove books to which they object. In 1985, a court case arose in Washington State when a student and her mother complained about a book the girl was assigned in her English class, Gordon Parks's coming-of-age novel *The Learning Tree.* The teacher agreed to assign an alternate book, but the mother and her daughter still filed suit in U.S. district court, claiming that the book violated their First Amendment religious rights by teaching secular humanism. Both the U.S. district court and the Ninth Circuit Court of Appeals ruled against the family, saying any infringement on the girl's constitutional rights was minimal because she had been given an alternative book to read.[52] A similar case took place in Tennessee, when a mother complained about a textbook that included a story about mental telepathy, which she said violated her religious beliefs. Her children were given an alternate textbook, but when the county school board voted to eliminate alternate reading assignments, she and other parents sued. One of the parents suing testified he objected to books that dealt with magic; role reversal or role elimination, particularly biographical material about women who have been recognized for achievements outside their homes; and emphasis on one world or a planetary society. A U.S. district judge ruled in favor of the parents and ordered that their children be given alternate reading assignments, but his ruling was overturned on appeal by the Sixth Circuit Court of Appeals, which stated that the children were not being coerced into declaring or believing religious beliefs that differed from their own and that the parents were trying to impose their own religious beliefs on the public school system.[53] As the appeals court decision stated:

It is clear that to the plaintiffs there is but one acceptable view—the Biblical view, as they interpret the Bible. Furthermore, the plaintiffs view every human situation and decision, whether related to personal belief and conduct or to public policy and programs, from a theological or religious perspective. Mrs. Frost [one of the plaintiffs] testified that many political issues have theological roots and that there would be "no way" certain themes could be presented without violating her religious beliefs. She identified such themes as evolution, false supernaturalism, feminism, telepathy and magic as matters that could not be presented in any way without offending her beliefs. The only way to avoid conflict with the plaintiffs' beliefs in these sensitive areas would be to eliminate all references to the subjects so identified. However, the Supreme Court has clearly held that it violates the Establishment Clause to tailor a public school's curriculum to satisfy the principles or prohibitions of any religion.[54]

About the same time as the Tennessee case was going on, a similar dispute erupted in Florida, but the outcome was quite different. The 1986 dispute over a textbook, involving the Christian Right, led to a court decision in Florida that appears to grant school officials greater latitude in pulling books out of classrooms and off library shelves. A minister in Lake City, Florida, objected when his daughter was assigned a textbook, *The Humanities: Cultural Roots and Continuities, Vol. 1,* which contained "The Miller's Tale" from Chaucer's *Canterbury Tales* and Aristophanes's play, *Lysistrata.* The minister complained about vulgar language "and the promotion of women's lib" in the book; in response, the school board, the majority of which had been elected on a campaign of restoring Christian values to the schools, voted to remove the text from the classroom and place it in a restricted area of the school library.[55] Both a U.S. district udge[56] and the 11th U.S. Circuit Court of Appeals[57] sided with the school board in *Virgil v. School Board,* citing the 1988 Supreme Court decision in *Hazelwood v. Kuhlmeier.*[58] That *Hazelwood* decision, which came in a high school newspaper censorship case, gave school officials greater authority to censor expression that is part of the curriculum, as long as the restrictions are pedagogically based. The conservative members of the school board were voted out of office in the next school board election, but Ralph Reed, at the time leader of the Christian Coalition, said conservative control of school boards—and the process by which books are adopted in schools—was one of his group's major goals.

Other lawsuits against the selection of books had different outcomes. The Ninth Circuit Court of Appeals ruled in 1994 against parents who were trying to force the school board to remove books they claimed violated their religious beliefs. That same year, the Seventh Circuit Court ruled against a parental challenge to another text.[59] In 1995, the Fifth Circuit Court of Appeals ruled against a group of parents who tried to force school officials to remove a book about voodoo from a school library.[60]

The Christian Right has not given up in its fight over books. The Christian Coalition, responding to the Republican Party's Contract with America in 1994 as the GOP regained control of Congress in the midterm election, created its own Contract with the American Family as a proposed guide for the new Congress. One of the planks of this platform was titled "Restoring Education Control to the Local Level" and contained the following language: "Parents are distressed over the failure of schools to teach children basic skills of reading, writing, and arithmetic. Too often, sex education emphasizes contraception rather than abstinence and self-control. Homosexuality is promoted as an acceptable alternative lifestyle."[61]

OBJECTIONS FROM THE LEFT

The inclination to censor is not found only among conservatives or among certain religious denominations. Censorship of books knows no political point of view. First Amendment scholar Nat Hentoff writes that the "lust to suppress can come from any direction."[62] African American protests have removed *Huckleberry Finn* from classrooms because of its language about blacks, and Jewish complaints have led to the removal of Shakespeare's *Merchant of Venice* because of its anti-Semitic content.[63]

Those on the left have been as adamant as those on the right in imposing their worldview on books, particularly textbooks. The Left believes books should reflect a tolerant world where differences are accepted, and books containing offensive images or words should be replaced. One organization that led the fight to ensure that textbooks did not use sexist or racist language or images was the Council on Interracial Books for Children, which was created in 1966 and existed until 1990. Its initial goal was to encourage publishers to include realistic and accurate stories about racial minorities, but its mission morphed into a campaign to persuade librarians to remove "offensive" books from their shelves—not only those that had racist or sexist material but also those that were biased in favor of whites. The council even persuaded the American Library Association, which had a long history of opposing censorship, to adopt a resolution in 1979 opposing racism and sexism in library holdings.[64]

Textbook publishers, buffeted by the Right and the Left, have been forced to produce texts that offend no one. One, Scott-Foresman-Addison Wesley, drafted a 161-page guideline for editors, authors, and illustrators that required them to give balanced representations of all religious groups, races, and genders as well as the elderly and the disabled. Illustrations had to include all types of people, tall and short, heavy and thin.[65]

CHILDREN'S BOOKS

Some objections to books for primary school students in the public schools are easy to dismiss, such as the 1992 incident in Colorado when a parent complained that Dr. Seuss books were hypnotic when read aloud and should be removed from the classroom.[66] But some objections to texts and library books have been based on legitimate complaints about sexually explicit or otherwise inappropriate content. A parent group called Women's Prayer and Action Group in Fayetteville, Arkansas, for instance, has been fighting to remove books from the public school libraries that group members believe are porno-graphic. Indeed, some of the books outlined on the group's Web site include graphic sexual descriptions, but the sections are taken in isolation, without regard for the context of the passages.

The depiction of homosexuality as an alternative lifestyle has raised the ire of parents throughout the country, who have fought to remove books such as *Heather Has Two Mommies* by Leslea Newman and *Daddy's Roommate* by Michael Willhoite. The fight over such books led to protracted wrangling in New York City in 1990, when the New York school board adopted a "rain-bow curriculum" that dealt with cultural diversity. Three years of argument ensued, with some of the New York borough school boards refusing to accept the curriculum. A watered-down version was finally approved.

More recently, legislators in at least two states—Oklahoma and Alabama—introduced bills that would restrict state funding for libraries that stock "pro-gay" books, although neither bill made it into law. The Wichita, Kansas, City Council voted in 1998, after a Baptist deacon complained about *Heather Has Two Mommies,* to require that if 300 library card holders signed a petition, a children's book could be moved into the adult section, although the rule was overturned in U.S. district court as unconstitutional.[67]

Like *Heather Has Two Mommies,* other children's books have undergone censorship not only because of language but also because of subject matter. One of most popular book series in the late twentieth and early twenty-first centuries, the Harry Potter books by J. K. Rowling, generates complaints that they promote witchcraft and are anti-Christian, or that they promote vio-lence.[68] For instance, school officials in Arkansas attempted to restrict access to the Harry Potter books in the school library to those who had permission slips from their parents, an effort struck down by a federal judge.[69]

Some Judy Blume books, including *Are You There God? It's Me, Marga-ret, Blubber,* and *Deenie* have been the subject of parental complaints—*Are You There, God?* because of its religious content, *Blubber* because a character engages in gross activity like picking his nose, and *Deenie* because a char-acter discusses masturbation.[70] Maurice Sendak's *In the Night Kitchen* was removed from libraries because it contains drawings that include a penis; in some libraries, the offending organ was whited out, or a diaper was drawn on.[71] Roald Dahl's *James and the Giant Peach* was banned in a Lufkin, Texas, elementary school because the word *ass* appears in it, and Maya Angelou's *I Know Why the Caged Bird Sings* was removed from the seventh- and eighth-grade reading lists at a New Hampshire school because it was considered to be sexually graphic.[72]

Library officials, despite the American Library Association's Bill of Rights, have also engaged in censorship. The library board in Camden, Missouri, removed all sex education books to the adult section in 1998 because the mother of an eight-year-old complained that he had checked out *Mommy Laid an Egg! Or, Where Do Babies Come From?*[73] Another children's sex education book, *It's Perfectly Normal,* was removed from the school library in Clover Park, Washington.[74]

THE PSYCHOLOGY OF BOOK CENSORSHIP

Some psychologists believe that the drive to censor children's books lies in the desire to protect not only the protester's own children but also the child within. Tom Moore, quoted in William Noble's book *Bookbanning in America,* says the censor is aware he or she can be corrupted by the material in the book, so that the effort to restrict the book is to protect the inner child. Another psychologist, Gary Margolis, says book banners are crying out for help, battling a sense of helplessness with regard to the power of the printed word. According to Margolis, there is a book banner in everyone.[75]

Diane Ravitch, in her book *The Language Police,* summarizes why censors in the schools, regardless of their political viewpoint, are doing a disservice to the students they are trying to protect: "The censorship that has spread throughout American education has pernicious and pervasive effects.... It restricts the language and ideas that may be reproduced in textbooks. It surely reduces children's interest in schoolwork by making their studies so deadly dull. It undermines our common culture by imposing irrelevant political criteria on the literature and history that are taught."[76]

Kristen Huston, writing in the *UMKC Law Review,* contends that fear and hidden agendas drive book censors, with both conservatives and liberals striving to prevent children from being exposed to discussions of sex, depictions of nudity, discussions of conflicts between science and religion (the conservative viewpoint), or depictions of sexism or racism (the liberal viewpoint): "It is one of the many ironies of the time that more than a few liberals and radicals found themselves with a foot in each camp, demanding freedom in one cause, censorship in another."[77]

COMIC BOOKS

Not only traditional books but also comic books have been the object of censors, and it took a U.S. Supreme Court decision to clear the way for many of these comics to be sold on the open market. Comic books were first sold on newsstands in 1933, and over the ensuing years many of them took on a racier and more violent tone, particularly after World War II. Critics began claiming that the comics were a bad influence, including ABC Radio, which broadcast a program in 1948 on "What's Wrong With the Comics."[78] Many of these comic books were lurid.

States began to regulate the sale of comics, leading to the Supreme Court decision in *Winters v. New York,* which concerned a book dealer who was convicted of selling true crime magazines that violated a New York state law forbidding the sale of any printed material "principally made up of criminal news, police reports, accounts of criminal deeds, or pictures, or stories of deeds of bloodshed, lust or crime."[79] The Court, noting that 20 other states had similar statutes, ruled all of them unconstitutional violations of the First Amendment, saying they were too vague in defining what was impermissible. Further, the Court ruled, comic books or other lurid publications could not be said to cause criminal activity because sociologists had been unable to pinpoint any single cause of such activity.

Despite the ruling in the *Winters* case, the effort to ban comics as harmful to America's youths was jump-started in 1954 when Dr. Fredric Wertham published a book, *Seduction of the Innocent,* detailing the ways he believed that comic books led to juvenile delinquency.[80] Wertham, a psychologist who worked at the New York City Department of Hospitals, contended in his book that comic books were a how-to course for juvenile delinquents. Part of his book was excerpted in the *Ladies Home Journal,* gaining widespread attention for his claims.[81] Wertham attributed all of society's ills to the media, particularly comics, making such overreaching claims as: "All of the child drug addicts, and all the children drawn into the narcotics traffic as messengers, with whom we have had contact were inveterate comic-book readers."[82]

Wertham's premise, that reading comic books led to juvenile delinquency, was based on an outdated theory of how media messages influence the consumer of that message. Wertham's contention was based on the "magic bullet" or "hypodermic needle" approach to media effects, which holds that media tell people how to think. This theory of media influence was discredited as oversimplified as early as the 1940s by researchers who determined that a much more complex multilevel model relying on personal experience and receipt of messages from other sources limited the direct effects of media.[83]

Regardless, Wertham gained much attention with his book. Estes Kefauver began a series of hearings in the Senate Subcommittee on Juvenile Delinquency, leading to a hearing by the Senate Judiciary Committee on the threat caused by comics. Among the witnesses was Wertham, who testified, "If it were my task, Mr. Chairman, to teach children delinquency, to tell them how to rape and seduce girls, how to hurt people, how to break into stores, how to do any known crime...I would have to enlist the crime comic book industry."[84]

Much in the way the movie industry moved to self-censorship, as detailed later in this book, the comic book publishers adopted a voluntary Comics

Authority Code in the 1950s. This action headed off any congressional action that would have imposed direct censorship of comic books. That does not mean, however, that direct censorship did not occur. The Stamford, Connecticut, police chief, Joe Kinsella, working with the local PTA, sent a letter to each newsstand in town listing titles of works that he considered obscene and instructing that the offending publications be removed from sale permanently. When some newsstand operators objected, Kinsella replied that he would use force if necessary.[85]

Censorship boards were established in cities across the country, and in 1938 the Catholic Church established the National Office for Decent Literature (NODL), based in Chicago. The NODL created committees to review printed work, including comic books. If a comic book was approved by a five-member review committee, and if six months later a different five-member committee approved a different issue of the same comic book, it was placed on an approved list. Comics were not approved if they violated one of several criteria, such as glorifying crime, describing how to commit crime, portraying sex facts offensively, holding lawful authority in disrespect, and featuring lewd or suggestive illustrations or photographs.[86]

Despite self-censorship and the NODL's attempt to censor comics, the 1960s and 1970s brought a willingness by some comics publishers to push the edge, and by the 1980s censorship of mainstream comics had essentially become a relic of an earlier time. One sign of the willingness of the comic book industry to fight censorship was creation of the Comic Book Legal Defense Fund, created in 1986 after the owner of a comic book store in Lansing, Michigan, was arrested for selling obscene comics, including the titles *The Bodyssey, Weirdo,* and *Bizarre Sex.* Other comic book sellers have been arrested since then on charges of selling obscene comics to adults or indecent comics to minors.[87]

CONCLUSION

Who is committing book censorship? Stephen Robinson, writing in the *English Journal,* cites two forces that lead to restrictions on books: the government, with its perception of what is best for the public, and "a second governing force made up of public opinion, community standards, and individual prejudices."[88] Eli M. Oboler cites group prejudice and fear of social change.[89] In some cases, a perfect storm of government officials, community leaders, and worried parents arises to turn legitimate criticism of a book or books into a sometimes-unstoppable move toward censorship.

The great playwright Arthur Miller, whose own plays such as *The Crucible* and *Death of a Salesman* faced censorship problems, writes, "Evidently there are many Americans who still do not understand that censorship and democracy cannot live happily together. What so many seem to forget is that a censor does not merely take something out, he puts something in, something of his own in a work that does not belong to him. His very purpose is to change a work to his own tastes and preconceptions."[90]

Whether operating from the Right or Left, censors attempt to force a particular social agenda on publishers. Censors, whether trying to remove books from school libraries, public libraries, or approved classroom reading lists, usually are trying to prevent social changes that they see as threatening their way of life or to force social changes through political correctness. When Kurt Vonnegut's book *Slaughterhouse-Five* is ordered to be removed from library shelves and class reading lists and one of the complaints is that the book is unpatriotic and godless, the censors are reacting to larger social issues. But when school officials remove *My Friend Flicka* because a female dog is called a bitch or *Belling the Tiger* because a church group complains that *bless me* as an expression is blasphemy, or when *Little Red Riding Hood* and *Hansel and Gretel* are attacked as sexist, it is harder to cite social changes as the reason.[91]

A further concern of authors, publishers, and librarians alike is the movement, once common but rejected in the appeals court's *Ulysses* decision, to judge the totality of a book by picking out isolated sections, what children's author Betty Miles called the trend toward "judging them as good or bad because of tone or general theme or overall effect."[92] A book that addresses homosexuality (*My Two Dads*) or social inequity (*The Grapes of Wrath*) or religion (*Are You There, God? It's Me, Margaret*) is condemned because of the subject matter with no regard for the literary quality of the book.

Those who favor restrictions on materials available in public schools or public libraries argue that their tax money should not support material they find offensive. Springfield, Virginia, resident Karen Jo Gounaud, for instance, became upset that her public library was distributing a free gay-oriented newspaper, *The Blade,* and she formed an organization called Family Friendly Libraries "to empower people at the local level...to determine what is done with their tax money and how their children are influenced" by what libraries purchase.[93]

The nation has a long history of censoring books, and despite complaints from both the Left and the Right, there is little doubt that censorship efforts in the schools and in public libraries will continue.

NOTES

1. Lynn Withrow, "Splinter Text Group Hits Prominent Writers' Works," *Charleston Daily Mail,* November 1, 1974.

2. "Kanawha PTA Board Opposes Certain Texts," *The Charleston Gazette,* June 19, 1974.

3. G. H. Hillocks Jr., "Books and Bombs: Ideological Conflict and the Schools—A Case Study of the Kanawha County Book Protest," *School Review* 86 (August 1978): 632–54.

4. Withrow, "Splinter Text Group."

5. C. A. Candor-Chander, "A History of the Kanawha County Textbook Controversy, April 1974–April 1975" (EdD diss., Virginia Polytechnic Institute and State University, 1976).

6. Yvonne Schiovani and Richard Haas, "Public Bus Drivers in Boycott," *Charleston Daily Mail,* September 10, 1974.

7. "U.S. Marshals to Enter Dispute," *The Charleston Gazette,* September 10, 1974.

8. "Minister 'Praying God Will Strike Dead,'" *Sunday Gazette-Mail,* September 29, 1974.

9. Kay Michael, "90,000 Textbooks Voted for Schools," *The Charleston Gazette,* November 9, 1974.

10. "School Officials Waive Hearing," *Charleston Daily Mail,* November 23, 1974.

11. A. L. Page and D. A. Clelland, "The Kanawha County Textbook Controversy: A Study of the Politics of Life Style Concern," *Social Forces* 57 (1978): 265–81, esp. 270.

12. Candor-Chander, "Kanawha County Textbook Controversy," 196.

13. William Noble, *Bookbanning in America: Who Bans Books and Why* (Middlebury, VT: Paul S. Eriksson, 1990), 58–68.

14. Nicholas J. Karolides, Margaret Bald, and Dawn B. Sova, *100 Banned Books: Censorship Histories of World Literature* (New York: Checkmark Books, 1999), 386–88.

15. Ibid., 278–80.

16. Ibid., 294–96.

17. Ibid., 327–30.

18. 72 F.2d 705 (2nd Cir. 1934).

19. Noble, *Bookbanning in America,* 69–78.

20. James R. Mock, *Censorship 1917* (Princeton, NJ: Princeton University Press, 1941), 153–54.

21. Ibid., 155–66.

22. Karolides, Bald, and Sova, 403.

23. Nat Hentoff, *Free Speech for Me But Not for Thee: How the American Left and Right Relentlessly Censor Each Other* (New York: HarperPerennial, 1992), 18–22.

24. Tim Hirsch, "Banned by Neglect: *Tom Sawyer,* Teaching the Conflicts," in *Censored Books II: Critical Viewpoints, 1985–2000,* ed. Nicholas Karolides (Lanham, MD: Scarecrow Press, 2002), 1–9.

25. Lee Buress, Nicholas J. Karolides, and John M. Kean, "Introduction," in *Censored Books: Critical Viewpoints,* ed. Nicholas Karolides, Lee Buress, and John M. Kean (Lanham, MD: Scarecrow Press, 1993), xii–xiv.

26. Dorothy Massie, "Censorship in the Schools," in *Censorship and Education,* ed. Eli M. Oboler (New York: H. H. Wilson, 1981), 78.

27. Noble, *Bookbanning in America,* 203.

28. Ibid.

29. James J. Martin, "Other Days, Other Ways: American Book Censorship 1918–1945," *Journal of Historical Review* 10, no. 2 (Spring 1990): 133–41.

30. Louise S. Robbins, *Censorship and the American Library: The American Library Association's Response to Threats to Intellectual Freedom, 1939–1969* (Westport, CT: Greenwood Press, 1996), 70.

31. Noble, *Bookbanning in America,* 204; see also James Alvino, "Is It Book Burning Time Again?" in Oboler, *Censorship and Education,* 32.

32. Hentoff, *Free Speech,* 2.

33. Bennett Cerf, "War and Book Business," *Publishers Weekly,* March 28, 1942, 1248.

34. Karolides, Bald, and Sova, 43–55.

35. Robbins, *Censorship and the Library,* 13.

36. Richard J. Peltz, "Pieces of *Pico:* Saving Intellectual Freedom in the Public School Library," *Brigham Young University Education and Law Journal* 2 (2005): 103–58, esp. 125–26.

37. Thomas Bowdler published a "family" version of Shakespeare's plays in a volume in which he attempted to excise anything he found offensive; this gave rise to the term *bowdlerizing* for attempting to censor a work of literature.

38. Karolides, Bald, and Sova, *100 Banned Books,* 374–76.

39. 175 F. Supp. 488 (S.D. NY 1959).

40. Karolides, Bald, and Sova, *100 Banned Books,* 299–303.

41. Ibid., 303–6.

42. Noble, *Bookbanning in America,* 171.

43. Nat Hentoff, *The First Freedom: The Tumultuous History of Free Speech in America* (New York: Delacorte Press, 1980), 26–35.

44. 457 U.S. 853 (1982).

45. Ibid. at 870–71.

46. James Hefley, *Are Textbooks Harming Your Children? Norman and Mel Galber Take Action and Show You How!* (Milford, MI: Mott Media, 1979), 9.

47. Noble, *Bookbanning in America,* 180–82.

48. Ibid., 183.

49. Walter H. Capps, *The New Religious Right: Piety, Patriotism, and Politics* (Columbia: University of South Carolina Press, 1990), 74–75.

50. Matthew Moen, "The Preacher versus the Teacher," *NEA Higher Education Journal* 9, no. 1 (1993): 125–43, esp. 139.

51. Sara Diamond, *Not by Politics Alone: The Enduring Influence of the Christian Right* (New York: Guilford Press, 1998), 174.

52. *Grove v. Mead School District No. 354,* 753 F.2d 1528 (9th Cir. 1985).

53. *Mozert v. Hawkins County Board of Education,* 827 F.2d 1058 (6th Cir. 1987).

54. Ibid. at 1064.

55. Karolides, Bald, and Soval, *100 Banned Books,* 360–61.

56. *Virgil v. School Board of Columbia County,* 677 F. Supp. 1547 (M.D. FL 1988).

57. *Virgil v. School Board of Columbia County,* 862 F.2d 1517 (11th Cir. 1988).

58. 484 U.S. 260 (1988). The *Hazelwood* case is discussed in chapter 6.

59. *Fleischfresser v. Directors of School District 200,* 15 F.3d 680 (7th Cir. 1994).

60. *Campbell v. St. Tammany Parish School Board,* 64 F.3d 184 (5th Cir. 1995).

61. "Christian Coalition Presents Contract with the American Family," in *The New Christian Right: Political and Social Issues,* ed. Melvin I. Urofsky and Martha May (New York: Garland, 1996), 198.

62. Hentoff, *Free Speech,* 1.

63. Ibid., 23.

64. Diane Ravitch, *The Language Police: How Pressure Groups Restrict What Students Learn* (New York: Alfred A. Knopf, 2003), 77–83.

65. Ibid., 35–36.

66. Barbara B. Gaddy, T. William Hall, and Robert J. Marzano, *School Wars: Resolving Our Conflicts over Religion and Values* (San Francisco: Jossey-Bass, 1996), 119.

67. Beverly C. Becker and Susan M. Stan, *Hit List for Children 2: Frequently Challenged Books* (Chicago: American Library Association, 2002), 60.

68. Robert Doyle, *Banned Books: 2000 Resource Guide* (Chicago: American Library Association, 2000), 1.

69. *Counts v. Cedarville School District,* 295 F. Supp. 2d 996 (W.D. AR 2003).

70. Robin F. Brancato, "In Defense of: *Are You There God? It's Me, Margaret, Deenie,* and *Blubber*—Three Novels by Judy Blume," in Karolides, Buress, and Kean, *Censored Books,* 87–97.

71. Mary Stolz, "White-Outs and Black-Outs on the Book Shelves," in Karolides, Buress, and Kean, *Censored Books,* 36.

72. Doyle, *Banned Books,* 1.

73. Becker and Stan, *Hit List for Children 2,* 6.

74. Ibid., 21.

75. Noble, *Bookbanning in America,* 155–56.

76. Ravitch, *Language Police,* 159–60.

77. Kristen Huston, "'Silent Censorship': The School Library and the Insidious Book Selection Censor," *UMKC Law Review* 72 (Fall 2004): 241–55, esp. 246.

78. Kenneth Paulson, "Regulation through Intimidation: Congressional Hearings and Political Pressure on America's Entertainment Media," *Vanderbilt Journal of Entertainment and Law Practice* 7 (Winter 2004): 61–89.

79. 333 U.S. 507 (1948).

80. Fredric Wertham, *Seduction of the Innocent* (Toronto: Clarke, Irwin & Co., 1954).

81. Paulson, "Regulation through Intimidation," 69.

82. Wertham, *Seduction of the Innocent,* 28.

83. Stanley J. Baran and Dennis K. Davis, *Mass Communication Theory: Foundations, Ferment and Future* (Belmont, CA: Wadsworth, 2000), 73.

84. Paulson, "Regulation through Intimidation," 71.

85. Robert W. Haney, *Comstockery in America: Patterns of Censorship and Control* (Boston: Beacon Hill Press, 1960), 86–87.

86. Ibid., 88–90.

87. Joseph Burton, "Sidebar 3—Censorship of Comic Books Challenged by Defense Fund," *Serials Review* 20, no. 4 (1994): 58.

88. Stephen Robinson, "Freedom, Censorship, Schools and Libraries," *English Journal* 70 (January 1981): 58–59.

89. Eli M. Oboler, "Introduction," in *Censorship and Education,* ed. Eli M. Oboler (New York: Wilson, 1981), 9.

90. Arthur Miller, "On Censorship," in Karolides, Buress, and Kean, *Censored Books,* 4.

91. Stolz, "White-Outs and Black-Outs," 32–40.

92. Noble, *Bookbanning in America,* 150.

93. Diamond, *Not by Politics Alone,* 188.

4

Censorship of Visual and Performing Arts

Motion pictures, dramatic works presented in theaters, art, and art photography convey a visceral content that some people find threatening. Almost from their beginnings in America, each of these art forms has encountered fear, official rebuke, and censorship. The censorship of movies was sanctioned by the U.S. Supreme Court in 1915.[1] One of the first attempts to stage a play in the British colonies (which later, of course, became the United States), by a group of students, was prevented by the government, which likened drama to the bacchanalia of Rome.[2] Both performances and recordings of music have faced censorship. Photography, although a newer art form compared to theater, has been censored when the images deal with sexual themes. Television has been subject to both external and self-censorship since its introduction into American life in the 1930s.

In some cases, the censorship takes the form of direct governmental action, with the artists subject to criminal charges, fines, and even time in jail for creating artistic works that offend those in power. In other cases, the censorship by government is more indirect, through legislation or officially authorized policies that subject creative works to review boards; in some of these situations, the artists, whether in film, theater, or other arts, must submit to censorship in order to present their works to an audience. Whether direct or indirect, the result of censorship is often the same—the creative effort must conform to an exterior force's vision of what is acceptable and unacceptable to the public at large to read, see, or hear.

MOVIES

Compared to books, newspapers, and paintings, motion pictures are a relatively recent phenomenon. Movies began as nickelodeons, where customers paid a few cents to watch a short, silent film. These nickelodeons were primarily located in storefronts and became immensely popular. By 1910, there were more than 10,000 such theaters in America.[3] City and state government officials, fearful that this new form of entertainment would corrupt the morals of their citizens, began enacting censorship codes to limit what could be displayed in motion pictures. Chicago enacted an ordinance in 1907 giving police the power to enforce morality in movies, and New York Mayor George B. McClellan ordered all movie theaters closed on Christmas Eve, 1908, as a threat to the city's morality, although the order was later rescinded.[4]

Two of the first states to enact movie censorship codes were Ohio and Kansas. Ohio created a state industrial commission with the authority to review and censor motion pictures, allowing only those that were of a "moral, educational or amusing or harmless character." The existence of this board was challenged by Mutual Film Corporation, which argued that censorship of movies violated its right to free speech. The U.S. Supreme Court did not agree. In its first ruling on motion picture censorship, in 1915 the Court ruled that movies were business ventures, not forms of free expression guaranteed by either the Ohio Constitution[5] or the First Amendment of the U.S. Constitution:[6] "It cannot be put out of view that the exhibition of moving pictures is business pure and simple, originated and conducted for profit, like other spectacles, not to be regarded by the Ohio Constitution, we think, as part of the press of the country or as organs of public opinions."[7]

In a case argued and decided at the same time as the Ohio case, the Supreme Court also upheld Kansas's movie censorship, as well as a tax levied on movies made elsewhere and brought into the state.[8] The Kansas law gave the state superintendent of public instruction authority to censor the movies, that is, to approve those that were "moral and proper and disapprove such as are sacrilegious, obscene, indecent or immoral, or such as tend to corrupt the morals."[9] The Supreme Court, referring to the Ohio case it decided the same day, said the Kansas law did not interfere with interstate commerce "nor abridge the liberty of opinion."[10]

In the years after these Supreme Court decisions cleared the way for cities and states to enact movie censorship codes, censorship boards and commissions flourished, yielding a confusing array of different local requirements and forbidden material. This worried the major studios; therefore, a number of them agreed to the formation of a National Board of Review by Charles Sprague Smith and the People's Institute, which, unlike many who viewed motion pictures as inherently evil, found them to be providing healthy entertainment.[11] A coalition of nine motion picture producers agreed to submit their films to this board, which would judge them on a national standard and suggest changes to each film.[12] This national review board began in 1915. It did not, however, stop the proliferation of state and city review boards. Self-censorship through the National Board of Review was not universally accepted, leading to two major changes in how movies were censored, the Hays Code and the Roman Catholic Church's Legion of Decency.

Critics called many motion pictures of the 1920s immoral and harmful to the viewing public. The Depression led to difficulties for many studios, with increases in production costs and a reduction in movie attendance from 90 million a week in 1930 to 60 million in 1933, with a corresponding reduction in the number of theaters that were open.[13] To draw a larger audience, the studios began relying on sex and violence in their films, leading to greater and greater calls for censorship. About the same time, a series of sex scandals rocked Hollywood, in particular, the suspicious death of a woman at a party hosted by obese comedian Roscoe "Fatty" Arbuckle,[14] the death of star Wallace Reid from drugs, and the divorce and immediate remarriage of "America's sweetheart," Mary Pickford.[15] In the face of renewed calls for censorship of motion pictures, a number of movie studio leaders formed the Motion Picture Producers and Distributors of America (MPPDA) and hired William "Will" Hays, the postmaster under President Warren Harding and chairman of the Republican National Committee, to be its public persona;[16] Joseph Breen was hired to put the new code into effect. In those roles, Hays and Breen began consolidating the local censorship rules into a national code. The Hays Code adopted rules designed to forestall any further state regulation of movies, among them a requirement that a synopsis of any proposed motion picture had to be forwarded to Hays's office and either approved, modified, or rejected.[17] Rejection could occur for any of a number of reasons. Depiction of immorality was acceptable so long as the sinners suffered and paid for their transgressions. Depiction of sexual conduct was also acceptable so long as it ended badly for all involved. Illegal traffic in drugs, profanity (including the words *hell* and *damn*), sexual perversion (defined by Breen as homosexuality), mixing of the races, ridicule of the clergy, and several other "immoral" actions or words were banned.[18] Breen and his cronies edited movie scripts line by line. Beginning in 1934, movies that were acceptable received a seal of approval.[19] The MPPDA was renamed the Motion Picture Association of America (MPAA) after World War II, but the censorship process remained. Appeals of MPAA rulings were rare: only six from 1954 to 1964.[20]

About the same time as Hays's office was developing its rules, the Catholic Church was initiating a separate movie censorship process as church leaders became concerned about the morals of Americans who were flocking to the movie theaters. This newest front in the censorship war began in Los Angeles in 1933 when Bishop John J. Cantwell asked the movie studios to engage in self-censorship. Meanwhile, Cardinal George Mundelein began his own inquiries into the best way to restore moral authority to motion pictures.[21] In part because of Mundelein's and Cantwell's efforts, the new apostolic delegate to the United States, Amleto Giovanni Cicognani, in his first speech in the United States roundly rebuked the motion picture industry, calling movies "a deadly menace to morals."[22] By 1934, the Catholic Church had created the Legion of Decency, requiring movie producers to submit their films to a small panel of reviewers in New York.[23] Those who did not submit to the church's censorship board risked the wrath of Catholic leaders across the country, who would require Catholics everywhere to boycott not only the offending films but also, for six months to a year, the theaters that showed the movies.[24] The Legion of Decency censors reviewed movies both for immorality and for adherence to Catholic tenets as well as criticism of the church. Among movies that were heavily censored by the Legion of Decency were classics such as *A Streetcar Named Desire, Lolita,* and *Suddenly Last Summer.*[25]

In addition, cities enacted codes requiring movies to meet local standards as well. United Artists, for instance, ran into a roadblock in Memphis, Tennessee, in 1949 when it attempted to distribute the movie *Curley,* a film that depicted the escapades of a group of white and African American children who are in school together. The city's board of censors—an organization that was common in many American cities at the time—refused to allow the movie to be shown at any of the city's theaters. The offense was that it depicted whites and African Americans attending the same school, an unconscionable act in the eyes of the board of censors. Lloyd Binford, the chair of the board of censors, had some idiosyncrasies; for instance, as a former railway clerk who was once robbed at gunpoint, he banned any movies that had "Jesse James" in the title. He once banned the movie *Stromboli* because its star, Ingrid Bergman, and its director, Roberto Rossellini, were living together without being married. So it was not out of character for Binford and his board of censors to prohibit the showing of a movie because it offended his sense of propriety involving the races.[26] As Binford wrote to United Artists, "I am sorry to have to inform you that it [the Board of Censors] is unable to approve your 'Curley' picture with the little negroes as the south does not permit negroes in white school nor recognize social equality between the races even in children."[27]

United Artists, the distributor of *Curley,* challenged the board of censors' decision in the Tennessee state courts. United Artists lost, both at trial and in the state Supreme Court, because the judges in the case ruled that United Artists was a "foreign" corporation (not based in Tennessee) and the local censorship board could be challenged only by an in-state company. The board of censors' decision was allowed to stand.[28]

Movie producers had, therefore, to endure separate but equally strict censorship processes: local codes, the Hays Code, and the Legion of Decency. Many chafed under this triple restriction. Two U.S. Supreme Court rulings, as well as the willingness of popular movie producers to ignore the Legion of Decency and Hays Code, led to the demise of both national codes, as well as the local codes. In 1948, the Supreme Court ruled in *U.S. v. Paramount Pictures*[29] that it was a violation of antitrust laws for the movie studios to own the theaters that showed their films, which led to the development of more independent movie theaters. The owners of some of these theaters were more willing to ignore the MPAA and the Legion of Decency and show controversial but artistic movies. Some of these movies, including *Who's Afraid of Virginia Woolf* and *The Pawnbroker,* with its stark depiction of the Holocaust including some nudity, did not win the approval of the Legion of Decency or the MPAA due to their mature subject matter and adult language, but they were commercial successes nonetheless, proving that movies did not have to have official approval from a self-appointed censorship board to bring in millions of dollars at the box office. Then, in 1952, the Supreme Court reversed its precedent in the 1915 *Mutual Film* case and ruled in *Burstyn v. Wilson* that motion pictures were in fact protected by the First Amendment.[30] In that case, the Court ruled that a New York law banning the showing of sacrilegious films violated the free speech clause of the First Amendment:

It cannot be doubted that motion pictures are a significant medium for the communication of ideas. They may affect public attitudes and behavior in a variety of ways, ranging from direct espousal of a political or social doctrine to the subtle shaping of thought which characterizes all artistic expression. The importance of motion pictures as an organ of public opinion is not lessened by the fact that they are designed to entertain as well as to inform....It is urged that motion pictures do not fall within the First Amendment's aegis because their production, distribution, and exhibition is a large-scale business conducted for private profit. We cannot agree. That books, newspapers, and magazines are published and sold for profit does not prevent them from being a form of expression whose liberty is safeguarded by the First Amendment.[31]

The Court noted in its decision, however, that it was not deciding whether the states were still free to outlaw obscene movies, a position the Court took in later cases and which is discussed more fully in chapter 5 in this book.

Gregory Black, in his book *The Catholic Crusade against the Movies: 1940–1975,* argues that it was the film *Who's Afraid of Virginia Woolf,* based on an Edward Albee play and starring Richard Burton and Elizabeth Taylor as a New England college professor and his wife with a bitter relationship, that most directly led to the demise of the Legion of Decency and the MPAA code that had been in effect since Hays's creation of the review process.[32] The Legion of Decency condemned the film, but it was a rousing success, with many Catholics ignoring the order to boycott the film. The Legion of Decency sputtered on for a few more years but officially was disbanded in 1980. At the same time, the MPAA had a new director, Jack Valenti, a former advisor to President Lyndon Johnson. Valenti, who was more liberal than the previous heads of the MPAA censorship operation, had no problem giving his approval to *Who's Afraid of Virginia Woolf.*[33]

In 1966, the MPAA, under Valenti's direction and with the cooperation of the National Association of Theater Owners, created a voluntary code system that indicated what age groups were appropriate to see each movie.[34] The ratings were G (general audience), M (mature audience), R (restricted for people under 16), and X (off-limits to minors). Over the years, the MPAA tinkered with the ratings system, finally coming up with the categories G (general audiences), PG (parental guidance suggested for younger audiences), PG-13 (recommended for viewers 13 and over, with parental guidance), R (restricted for viewers under 17 without parent or guardian present), and NC-17 (no one under 17 admitted). With the adoption of this coding system, the era of movie censorship by independently created groups such as the Legion of Decency ended.

THE THEATER

Censorship of dramatic productions is as old as the country itself. As soon as they landed in the New World, the Puritans, who believed that anything that was not holy was sacrilegious, banned almost all plays. In 1634 they also banned mixed-sex dancing, the celebration of Christmas (because the Bible did not specify on what date Christ was born), or the purchase of clothing decorated with silk, gold, or lace.[35] The first play written in English and performed in the colonies was *Ye Bare and Ye Cubb.* Government officials charged the actors with acting in a play, but they were acquitted.[36] After this, the presentation of plays grew in number in the colonies and faced little in the way of official opposition until a group of actors attempted to stage a production in Boston (primarily Puritan) in 1750, prompting the General Court of Massachusetts to enact a law banning plays and fining anyone who allowed his property to be used for a theatrical production.[37] A number of other colonies followed suit, and soon actors were forced to hide their theaters under the names of "lectures" or "schools" to evade the laws.[38]

The widespread official condemnation of the theater as immoral prompted the new Congress of the United States to pass a law in 1778 stating that anyone who acted in, encouraged, or attended a play would be considered unfit for federal office.[39] The law had little effect, especially since new President George Washington was an avid theatergoer. In the 1790s theaters were closed for a time in New York and Boston because of an outbreak of yellow fever and at other times because the crowds were too rowdy.[40]

The fear of theater as an immoral force continued into the nineteenth century. For example, an attempt to open a theater in Lowell, Massachusetts, led to the arrest of several actors for pursuing an unlawful profession.[41] By the 1850s, state legislators began to enact laws giving the states the power to license theaters and performances, often delegating that authority to local officials. The greatest threat, according to these laws, was not the productions themselves but the unruly audiences. These laws had the effect of turning the theater into a middle-class attraction and popularizing plays.[42]

In March 1900, New York City officials shut down a play, a production of *Sappho,* which included, among other things, a scene in which a woman is carried up a flight of stairs by her lover; the curtain was lowered and then raised, with the stage lighting indicating the passage of time from night to dawn—clearly, Sappho had spent the night in bed with a man to whom she was not married. William Randolph Hearst, the editor of the *New York Journal,* editorialized that the play was immoral and corrupting, and police responded by arresting the lead actress, Olga Nethersole, for corrupting public morals, and closed the play. She eventually was tried and acquitted, and the play resumed a month later.[43]

Censorship of plays by local officials continued throughout the 1900s. *The Lure,* a play about a young woman tempted to work in a brothel, was closed by New York City in 1913,[44] and the New York district attorney's office impaneled a grand jury to investigate whether a number of dramatic productions were objectionable (the jurors recommended changes to some plays to make them tamer).[45] The district attorney succeeded in shutting down one play temporarily, Eugene O'Neill's *Desire Under the Elms,* in which a wife had an out-of-wedlock son with her stepson, then killed the child so that she would inherit the family farm. After the jurors recommended the play not be altered, it was allowed to reopen. But the play did run into problems elsewhere: it was banned in Boston, and the cast was arrested in Los Angeles because the play was judged obscene.[46]

Perhaps the most noteworthy censorship incident started in 1926 when the notorious actress Mae West penned a play titled *Sex,* which portrayed a prostitute whose life turns out well. The next year, after sellout crowds led to an extension of the play into the next season, Deputy Police Commissioner Joseph McKee took the opportunity of the mayor's trip out of town to conduct a raid on the play and arrest West and her entire cast. After a night in jail, West paid the $100 bail for the six principal actors and $500 for each of the 16 other cast members, and they were released. West refused the court's offer to drop the charges if she would cancel the play. West, the theater owner, her manager, her lawyer, and 20 actors were indicted for producing an obscene, lewd, wicked, scandalous, and indecent play that corrupted the morals of minors. West and her lawyer were convicted, fined $500 each, and sentenced to 10 days in jail, but the charges against the owner and the actors were dropped. West arrived at the prison in a limousine and carried a bouquet of white roses. After her incarceration, she told reporters she had worn silk underwear and had dined with the warden and his wife; she later was paid $1,000 to give a magazine interview and used the proceeds to fund the Mae West Memorial Library at the prison.[47]

Censorship continued to plague play producers and actors in cities from Philadelphia to Boston to Los Angeles. Among noted playwrights whose work was censored were Eugene O'Neill (*Strange Interlude,* which had themes of adultery and abortion), the ancient Greek Aristophanes (*Lysistrata,* in which Greek women are urged not to sleep with their husbands until the men ended a war), and Lillian Hellman (*The Children's Hour,* which included lesbianism).[48] New York's legislature passed a bill in 1937 giving a city the power to revoke the performance permit for a play considered to be immoral, but the governor vetoed it under pressure from actors, producers, and writers.[49]

The federal government became involved in limiting the production of dramatic works in the 1930s when the Works Progress Administration (WPA), part of President Franklin Delano Roosevelt's New Deal, became involved in producing plays. The WPA formed the Federal No. 1 initiative, which would use federal funding to hire artists, musicians, writers, and theater personnel; included in this program was the Federal Theater Project, which was supposed to create noncommercial theater projects. One play, *The Cradle Will Rock,* which depicted a labor union victory over a vicious capitalist, was blocked by Federal Theater Project officials. The producers, John Houseman and Orson Welles, managed to stage a minimal version without the sets and costumes, which had been padlocked in the original theater where it had been scheduled.[50]

Attempts to silence plays continued in cities throughout the rest of the twentieth century. The exotic belly dancer who appeared in the comedy *Fanny* was ordered by police in 1954 to wear a less-revealing outfit. Tennessee Williams's classic play *Cat on a Hot Tin Roof* brought an objection by the New York City Commissioner of License, who ordered some offensive language eliminated from the production before it could continue. Baylor University, a Baptist-affiliated school in Texas, banned Eugene O'Neill's *Long Day's Journey into Night* in 1962 because it was in bad taste.[51]

As tastes and public perceptions of morality began to change in the turbulent 1960s, censorship of plays lessened but did not end. Los Angeles police filed obscenity charges, later dropped, against *The Toilet,* a play that takes place in a dingy bathroom at an urban high school and explicitly deals with homosexuality.[52] One of the more controversial productions during this period was the countercultural musical *Hair,* which included cast nudity and controversial sexual topics. U.S. army officials banned the production from army bases, whereas city officials in Indianapolis, South Bend, Indiana, Evansville, Indiana, St. Paul, Minnesota, and San Antonio, Texas, ordered that nudity in the production be eliminated. Censorship in Chattanooga, Tennessee, prompted a theater production company to sue in U.S. district court, but the court ruled that the nudity and simulated sex in *Hair* were not speech and was not protected by the First Amendment, a decision upheld on appeal by the Sixth Circuit Court of Appeals.[53] The plaintiffs then appealed to the U.S. Supreme Court, which overturned the lower courts and ruled in *Southeastern Promotions Ltd. v. Conrad* that censorship of the production was prior restraint prohibited by the First Amendment:

Only if we were to conclude that live drama is unprotected by the First Amendment— or subject to a totally different standard from that applied to other forms of expression—could we possibly find no prior restraint here.... By its nature, theater usually is the acting out—or singing out—of the written word, and frequently mixes speech with live action or conduct. But that is no reason to hold theater subject to a drastically different standard.[54]

Nonetheless, prior restraint of plays continued. In 1989, a production of *Equus,* which includes male nudity, was reviewed by police before it could be performed in public.[55] In 1965, attempts by police in San Francisco and Berkeley, California, to arrest performers in *The Beard,* which showed simulated oral sex, were overturned by a California court, which ruled that police could not ban plays that were not legally obscene under Supreme Court guidelines.[56] Despite this and other rulings, efforts to restrict what can be presented persist. Even when there was no nudity on stage, play content could still lead to censorship. The production *The President Is Dead,* concerning the assassination of President Lincoln, was banned in 1969 from Ford's Theater, where the assassination had occurred in 1865, because the theater board thought its subject matter inappropriate.[57] A book that contained *Lysistrata* was pulled from a school library in Lake City, Florida, in 1999 because some parents complained it promoted "women's lib" and contained pornography. That same year a performance of *West Side Story,* the tale of love and gangs in New York, was canceled because Hispanic students said the play reflected stereotypes about Puerto Ricans.[58] A performance by the Wentworth Institute of Technology drama club of *The Best Little Whorehouse in Texas* was canceled in 1997 because the dean of students said the title would be inappropriate to list in an alumni newsletter.[59]

Plays and musicals can also run afoul of religious sensibilities. One conservative author called *Jesus Christ Superstar,* a rock musical retelling of the life of Christ, "blasphemous, sacrilegious, desecrating, apostate, and anti-Christian."[60] When the Springfield, Missouri, Little Theater put on *The Full Monty* in 2006, with the male actors appearing in underwear rather than nude as in the Broadway version, one of the actors had to resign his position as an adjunct professor at Evangel University because the Assemblies of God–affiliated school objected to his appearance in the play. University spokesman Paul Logsdon said performing in shows like *The Full Monty* violated Evangel's personnel policy: "There are just certain places, activities and forms of entertainment that we ask our students to abstain from, and the faculty and staff are held to the same standard."[61]

VISUAL ART

Censorship of visual art is almost as old as recorded history, dating to Egyptian art in the Third Dynasty, 3400–2900 B.C.[62] The histories of Europe and Asia are replete with examples of artists running afoul of the government and either being punished for their art or having their artworks seized. Censorship of painting and sculpture was rampant in Europe in the fifteenth through seventeenth centuries, but in what eventually became the United States, the first recorded instance of destruction of an artwork occurred in 1776, when a group of colonial soldiers pulled down a statue of King George III in New York City following news of the signing of the Declaration of Independence; four months later British soldiers retaliated by decapitating a statue of the Earl of Chatham, an advocate of the independence of the new nation, also in New York.[63] John Turnbull was hired to paint four large pictures in the U.S. capitol rotunda but then fired because of objections to what he included and what he omitted in the first of the four paintings.[64] Despite the political nature of these acts, most censorship of art during the early years of the United States focused, not surprisingly, on the depiction of the nude human body. In 1815, Jesse Sharpless was convicted of violating moral decency by possessing what the Court ruled was "a certain lewd, wicked, scandalous, infamous and obscene painting" depicting a man in an "indecent posture" with a woman.[65] In 1842, Congress enacted the United States Tariff Law, which banned the importation into the country of indecent or obscene pictorial works, the first time an antiobscenity law concerned strictly the visual arts. The next year, a shipment of snuff boxes containing nude paintings (hidden in a shipment of toys) was confiscated under this law.[66] The law was amended in 1857 to include indecent sculpture and photography, the first federal law in the United States regulating photography (although indecent or obscene photographs had been banned in England as early as 1847).[67] Antipornography crusader Anthony Comstock helped to persuade Congress to enact a law, known as the Comstock Act, giving the post office the authority to ban indecent material, including paintings, drawings, and photographs, from the mail and make possession of these materials a federal crime.[68] In a case arising out of the Comstock Act, August Miller was convicted in 1882 in New York of possessing obscene photographs, even though the photos were of paintings.[69] Also in 1882, the governor of Massachusetts recommended that the state normal school, where prospective teachers were being educated, be abolished because art students were making nude clay figures.[70] In a similar incident in 1890, an art class at the Art Students' League in New York was canceled because board members found it intolerable to have both male and female students enrolled in a drawing class in which nude models were being sketched.[71] It was not only students, however, that ran into trouble with depictions of nudity. In 1906, Comstock seized and destroyed an issue of *The American Student of Art* because it contained student drawings of nudity.[72] Chicago police in 1913 ordered the removal from a store window of a reproduction of the Paul Chabas painting "September Morn," depicting a young girl bathing nude on a lakeshore, but a jury later ordered it returned because it was not obscene.

Throughout the 1900s, similar isolated efforts at restricting painting and sculpture continued. The Oakland, California, library board, reacting to a display of nudes in paintings from Europe, decided in 1928 that all future art exhibits in the Oakland Art Museum, owned by the library, would have to be approved before they could be shown.[73] After *Life* magazine published a two-page photo display in 1938 showing nuns in their habits drawing a scantily clad male model at the Art Institute of Chicago, the nuns nearly had to withdraw from the school and were able to remain enrolled only after the dean wrote a letter of apology to the cardinal.[74]

Not only painting and sculpture but also the relatively new art of photography was raising the ire of some, particularly in a political sense during the red scare of the 1940s and 1950s. A number of photographers encountered trouble because of the subjects of their work—the poor and labor union members. Many were accused of being un-American, Communists, Communist sympathizers, socialists, or all of the above. A group of photographers who organized as the Photo League were included in 1947 in a list of "totalitarian, fascist, communist or subversive" organizations by U.S. Attorney General Tom Clark.[75] At about the same time, the U.S. House Public Works Committee began an investigation into what the chair perceived to be Communist influence in modern art, although he failed to persuade Congress to begin a full-scale investigation.[76] Nudity in photography also prompted official censorship. As early as 1888, Comstock argued that photographs of nude art were themselves obscene.[77] Eastman Kodak officials, worried about federal obscenity laws prohibiting the mailing of sexual images, established their own review process at their processing facilities, refusing to mail developed film or photographs without an explanation of how the photos were taken, even if the photographs were of well-respected paintings.[78]

Anti-Communism crusaders also attacked paintings that depicted what they considered to be improper topics. Two murals by Jose Clemente Orozco, for instance, were censored at New York's New School for Social Research—one covered, the other rejected—because they had depicted Lenin's face and had Gandhi and anti-imperialism as themes. A fellow Mexican immigrant and painter, David Alfaro Siqueiros, had a mural he painted for the Plaza Art Center in Los Angeles whitewashed.[79]

Besides paintings and photographs sculpture also ran afoul of the censors. The owner of a San Francisco art gallery was arrested, tried, and eventually acquitted after a nine-day trial in 1964 on a charge that he and his salesman were peddling obscenity by offering lewd objects for sale—11 sculptures made from junked automobile parts converted to depict sexual activity.[80] Marcel Fort, a Miami, Florida, sculptor, was arrested and fined $100 in 1967 for displaying in his yard, for the general public to see, a sculpture of a nude man and woman entwined in a sexual embrace.[81] A sculpture titled "The Spirit of '76," which included an American flag, a dynamite box, a Molotov cocktail, and a red flag, was removed from exhibition at the Minnesota State Fair in 1970, even though judges in a fair competition had awarded it an honorable mention. The police chief of New Orleans ordered a nude statute in the lobby of the new police department headquarters covered in 1968.[82] Lest anyone think this was an isolated incident, note that newly appointed U.S. Attorney General John Ashcroft ordered a nude statue of justice in the Justice Department covered when he took office in 2001.

Beginning in the 1960s, the battle over art turned in large part to the question of government funding of painting, photography, and sculpture. Congress created the National Endowment for the Arts (NEA) in 1965 as a method for ensuring that the arts in this country remained vital. Almost immediately, critics began to complain about taxes (in the form of government spending) being used to subsidize art that is offensive to the general public. Two of the most publicized examples of this objection to funding of controversial art involved photographs, both of which resulted in governmental action.

The first of these incidents concerned a 1987 photograph by Andres Serrano titled "Piss Christ," depicting a crucifix in a jar of urine.[83] It was one of eight works in a 1988 traveling show funded by the NEA and the Southeastern Center for Contemporary Art. When the show reached Richmond, Virginia, opposition to Serrano's photo was growing, fueled in part by the Reverend Donald Wildmon and his American Family Association, whose letter-writing campaign called the photo sacrilegious and an affront to Christians. The protest caught the attention of lawmakers in Washington, D.C., with Senator Jesse Helms calling it abhorrent and Senator Alphonse D'Amato calling it filth.[84] Helms, in his autobiography, argued that the federal government had no business financially supporting "an assault on America's basic values" with "a level of perversion that the NEA has previously funded as 'art.' "[85]

About the same time, a separate photography exhibit partly funded by the NEA was causing problems in Cincinnati, Ohio, and Washington, D.C. Robert Mapplethorpe's critically acclaimed series of photographs with homoerotic themes, some with white and black men posed together, prompted police to shut down the show; the prosecutor in Cincinnati charged the director of the city's Contemporary Arts Center, Dennis Barrie, with pandering obscenity, although Barrie was acquitted by a jury of the charges in 1990.[86]

Meanwhile, performance artist Karen Finley, who had received NEA grants in 1984, 1987, and 1989, drew attention from critics for her performances in which she covered her nude body with chocolate syrup and screamed about indignities visited upon women and people with AIDS.[87]

The controversy over the photographs by Serrano and Mapplethorpe, and Finley's performance art, was a perfect storm for opponents of NEA funding of offensive art. Members of Congress began to debate whether NEA funding for the arts was good stewardship of tax money, particularly if the money was used to fund deeply offensive material. After spending the summer of 1990 debating the value of the NEA, Congress voted to cut NEA funding by the amount that had been used for the Serrano and Mapplethorpe exhibits and also amended the NEA's charter, requiring the agency to ensure that "artistic excellence and artistic merit are the criteria by which [grant] applications are judged, taking into consideration general standards of decency and respect for the diverse beliefs and values of the American public." This new policy, aimed at preventing the NEA from funding obscene art, was challenged by Finley and other performance artists whose work had run afoul of NEA guidelines. The Supreme Court upheld the NEA's funding restrictions in 1998 as only minimal restrictions on the artists' free speech rights.[88]

Public funding of art has continued to be a hot topic for both artists and politicians. In 1998, for example, the Brooklyn Museum encountered opposition from Catholic groups and New York Mayor Rudy Giuliani when it exhibited a work by Chris Ofili titled "The Holy Virgin Mary," depicting a Black Madonna shellacked with elephant dung on her breasts. Giuliani threatened to close the museum and cut off its city funding if the offensive piece, which he called "sick stuff," was not removed. Museum officials went to federal court and won a ruling that the mayor's threat was censorship.[89]

CENSORSHIP OF MUSIC

When a number of women, including Tipper Gore, the wife of future vice president Al Gore, formed the Parents Music Resource Center (PMRC) in 1985, they touched off a debate over the nature of rock music and the effect some of that music has on the young people who listen to it. The PMRC was concerned about music lyrics that the group said touted the use of drugs and alcohol, promoted sexual activity, and encouraged the occult or violence. Gore cited her own purchase in 1984 of Prince's "Purple Rain" album for her 11-year-old daughter and her ensuing shock at lyrics about masturbation and other "vulgar lyrics." Gore began listening to other popular albums and watching music videos, including Van Halen's "Hot for Teacher," in which an attractive teacher does a striptease for her students.[90]

Gore and the other women who formed the PMRC began conducting public meetings and calling for mandatory labeling of recorded music. Gore contended that the warning label proposal "was the direct opposite of censorship. We called for more information, not less. We did not argue for a ban of even the most offensive albums or tapes. We simply argued that the consumer be forewarned through the use of warning labels and/or printed lyrics visible on the outside packaging of music products."[91] Many of those in the rock music field did not agree with Gore's characterization.

By 1985, Congress became involved when the U.S. Senate convened a subcommittee hearing to examine the PMRC's proposal; it may have been a coincidence, but Senator Al Gore was a member of the subcommittee. The hearing brought out several big-name musicians, including Frank Zappa, who had formed the group Mothers of Invention, and Dee Snider, lead singer for the group Twisted Sister. A *Washington Post* reporter called it a circus atmosphere, and Zappa called the PMRC's labeling proposal "the equivalent of treating dandruff with decapitation." "Taken as a whole," Zappa said, "the complete list of PMRC demands reads like an instruction manual for some sinister kind of 'toilet training' to housebreak all composers and performers because of the lyrics of a few. Ladies, how dare you."[92]

The PMRC had criticized the Twisted Sister song "Under the Blade" for espousing bondage and rape, but Snider, who described himself as a 44-year-old father of two who does not smoke, drink, or do drugs, called that allegation "slanderous" and "little more than character assassination," contending the song was meant to describe fear of surgery. He said the video for the song

"We're Not Going to Take It," rather than advocating anarchy, was cartoonish and "based on my extensive personal collection of Roadrunner and Wile E. Coyote cartoons."[93]

Even mainstream recording artist John Denver testified before the committee that his song "Rocky Mountain High" was banned by some radio stations because some believed it was about getting high on drugs, instead of celebrating the outdoors. As if summarizing the enduring fight over music and censorship, Denver said, "That which is denied becomes that which is most desired, and that which is hidden becomes that which is most interesting."[94] One of the subcommittee members, Senator Fritz Hollings of South Carolina, who, like Senator Gore, is married to a PMRC member, called the music discussed at the hearing "outrageous filth" and added, "If I could find some way constitutionally to do away with it, I would."[95]

In the end, the PMRC's record-labeling proposal ended with some record companies adopting voluntary labeling, and the PMRC's most visible member, Tipper Gore, resigned from the group when her husband was elected vice president in 1992. The episode, which attracted national media attention, was more sound and fury than action. It illustrates the passions, however, that can erupt whenever anyone proposes restrictions on what others can hear.

All types of music have run afoul of censors and would-be censors throughout history. Ancient Greek philosopher Socrates argued that musical innovations threatened established order.[96] In this nation's history, from folk songs to classical music, there has been something to offend someone. Big-band swing music, for instance, was seen as vastly inferior to classical music in the pre–World War II era, and jazz was banned from many radio stations because of its origins among African Americans in places such as Chicago and New Orleans. Even in the jazz world, critics complained about new styles of playing; bebop musicians such as trumpeter Dizzy Gillespie and saxophonist Charlie Parker were accused of making noise rather than playing music. Modern folk music has been called a tool of the Communists: author David A. Noebel, in his book *The Marxist Minstrels,* writes, for instance, "The Communist infiltration into the subversion of American music has been nothing short of phenomenal and in some areas, e.g. folk music, their control is fast approaching the saturation point."[97]

CENSORSHIP OF ROCK

But the history of music censorship has to focus on the development of rock in the 1950s and 1960s and the accompanying outcry over lyrics and, in the case of Elvis Presley and his swiveling pelvis, the movements. Rock began with performers such as Buddy Holly, Jerry Lee Lewis, and Chuck Berry reacting to the conservative 1950s, with its bomb shelters and the Eisen-hower administration's conservative policies. By the 1960s, when morality had begun to shift, many youngsters, part of the baby boom generation, began to experiment more with their music and lyrics.[98] Elvis scandalized the country when he performed his hip-swiveling music on the *Ed Sullivan Show,* and Roman Catholic Church leaders in Boston urged that rock music be banned.[99] Many critics saw what they wanted to see. Soviets saw rock as a sign of U.S. decadence, whereas anti-Communists saw rock as a sign of Soviet influence in America.[100]

One of the earliest venues for the national broadcast of rock was CBS's *Ed Sullivan Show,* which had a weekly audience of about 40 million; depending on the acts that were performing, the program was a must-watch for many Americans. The Beatles, for instance, made their American television debut on Ed Sullivan's show, attracting an audience of 74 million.[101] Performers ap-pearing on Sullivan's variety show had to deal not only with CBS's censors but Sullivan's as well. When Bob Dylan was told he could not perform his song "Talkin' John Birch Society Blues," satirizing the right-wing anti-Communist group, he walked out and refused to perform. The Rolling Stones band was ordered to change the lyrics of the band's hit "Let's Spend the Night Together" to "Let's spend some time together" because of the sexual connotation of the original lyrics. The Doors were told to change the lyrics of their hit "Light My Fire" from "girl, we couldn't get much higher" because of the drug con-notations; although the group agreed and actually sang different lyrics during rehearsal, lead singer Jim Morrison reverted to the original lyrics during the live broadcast. A furious Sullivan banned the group from his show after that 1967 performance.[102]

As the 1960s continued, the message of drugs, sex, and rebellion became more blatant in many songs. The Beatles, who began their careers singing songs like "I Wanna Hold Your Hand," began singing songs like "Lucy in the Sky with Diamonds," a not-too-oblique reference to LSD. The Doors' song "The End" was a lengthy Oedipal tale that ends with the narrator killing his father and having sex with his mother. Following the 1970 Kent State shoot-ings, in which four protesting students were shot to death, the group Crosby, Stills, and Nash recorded "Ohio," which included the refrain, "Nixon's com-ing, and four dead in Ohio."

Among those who objected to the new political, sexual, and drug-related content of rock were President Nixon, whose tastes ran to classical and coun-try music, and his vice president, Spiro Agnew. The vice president gave speech after speech in which he attacked the "long hairs" who were "brainwashing" American youths and lectured people to remain morally strong (ironically, Agnew later resigned from the vice presidency as part of a no-contest plea to corruption charges, and Nixon resigned because of his role in the Watergate cover-up).

The Federal Bureau of Investigation (FBI), under J. Edgar Hoover, conducted investigations of a number of musicians, including Janis Joplin, Jimi Hendrix, Jim Morrison, and Elvis Presley. Hendrix's file noted his arrest record on drug charges, and Joplin's file focused on her appearance at a concert in Chicago in 1970 because of the perceived threat of violence. Morrison's lengthy file includes a letter from a private citizen; Hoover's response was that "this type of recording...is repulsive to right-thinking people and can have serious effects on our young people."[103]

Another government method of regulating music has been to prohibit concerts or to prosecute musicians for their actions during the concerts. Jim Morrison, lead singer for the Doors, was infamously arrested during a 1970 concert in Miami, Florida, for reportedly exposing himself. Country Joe MacDonald, lead singer of the group Country Joe and the Fish, was fined $500 in Worcester, Massachusetts, in 1970, for leading a concert audience in an antiwar cheer that included a profanity. The Jefferson Airplane group and other bands were frequently forced to post bonds that would be forfeited if they violated rules.[104] In one infamous incident, the permit for an antiwar concert scheduled in Washington, D.C., prior to the May Day antiwar rally in 1971, was revoked at the direction of U.S. Attorney General John Mitchell and his assistant, future chief justice William Rehnquist. Some 70,000 concertgoers were ordered to leave the concert venue or face arrest. More recently, shock-rock musician Marilyn Manson's antics, including shouted obscenities and the destruction of Bibles, prompted a number of cities and states to consider laws requiring that concerts be equipped with parental warning labels, much as music and some videos are.[105]

The PMRC hearings into rock may have been the most publicized congressional look at music, but it was not the first. Senator James Buckley, a Republican from New York, had his staff examine the role of drugs in rock, and his November 1973 report called the "rock culture" the "drug culture," with musicians using drugs and promoting drugs in their lyrics and personal statements. The senator blamed rock for leading young people to drugs, but recording industry officials noted that people were using drugs long before the rock era.[106]

Not only congresspeople and parental activists but also corporate America became engaged in the business of censoring music. Wal-Mart, for example, refuses to stock music whose contents or even cover art it finds offensive, such as Sheryl Crow's self-titled album in 1996, because the lyrics to "Love Is a Good Thing" include the words "Watch our children as they kill each other with a gun they bought at the Wal-Mart discount stores."[107] Singer Jill Sobule complained in 1997 that Wal-Mart refused to stock her "Happy Town" CD because the cover depicted a Prozac pill being broken over a house; Wal-Mart officials said it was a drug reference.[108] In general, Wal-Mart will not carry CDs with cover art or lyrics that the company determines to be overtly sexual or that deal with abortion, homosexuality, or Satanism; as a result, many recording companies change cover art to appease the retail giant.[109]

In addition to rock, rap and hip-hip music have also come under fire for lyrics that critics say promote violence and denigrate women. In some cases, this urban music has been banned from television because of its content. One company official at Houston-based Rap-a-Lot Records said he had to edit rap videos because "otherwise, they wouldn't get played." An official at a music video channel, The Box, stated that videos are judged case-by-case, and those that are considered to be offensive because of language or use of a weapon are not aired. According to MCA Records' national director of video promotion, television networks have become more reluctant to air violent or sexual videos.[110]

Some local officials have attempted to engage in censorship of music, most notably with the group 2 Live Crew. The prosecutor in Alexander City, Alabama, charged local record store owner Tommy Hammond with distributing obscenity for selling 2 Live Crew's album "More Somethin'." He was convicted by a municipal judge but appealed to circuit court, where he was acquitted.[111] The Guilderland, New York, police chief sent a letter to local music stores warning them not to sell recordings that had content warning labels, ignoring the fact that these records were not obscene.[112]

RADIO AND TELEVISION

In the wake of the sinking of the Titanic in the icy North Atlantic, in which the ship's distress calls were not heard by radio operators who had ceased operations for the night, Congress in 1912 passed the first law regulating the fledgling field of broadcasting. The Radio Act of 1912 required all radio transmitters and operators to be licensed but gave the U.S. Commerce Secretary, future president Herbert Hoover, no authority to deny a license to anyone. The first commercial radio station in America was KDKA in Pittsburgh, Pennsylvania, which began broadcasting in 1920; hundreds more developed during the 1920s. As radio became more and more popular, radio stations began broadcasting without limits on the power of their signals or the frequencies they used. The result was chaos, with radio owners unable to listen to some of their favorite programs without hearing interference from other stations. This upset not only the radio listeners but also the radio manufacturers, who could foresee a decrease in demand for new radios.

As a result, Hoover called a series of meetings of those in the radio business, resulting in the federal Radio Act of 1927, which established the principles that the airwaves used by broadcasters to send out their signals belonged to the public and that anyone enjoying the benefits of a broadcast license had to serve the public's interest. That 1927 act was refined when Congress created the Federal Communications Commission (FCC) through the Federal Communications Act of 1934, which gave this federal agency the authority to regulate communication via radio and wire. The FCC used this authority to exert its control over radio as well as the new medium of television. Even though the act also expressly prohibited the FCC from censoring broadcasts, it gave the agency the power to determine which potential broadcast outlets could receive an FCC license.

The first regular television broadcast to a public audience took place in April 1939, and by 1958 there were 50 million television sets in America.[113] Unlike the other forms of visual and performing art, there has been little question over the years that the federal government has a role in regulating content of broadcasting, despite the ban on censorship. From 1949, when it was created, until 1987, when the FCC abolished it as part of the Reagan presidency's deregulation movement, the fairness doctrine required broadcasters to devote part of their programming to discussions of public interest matters and to give airtime for a response by members of the public who disagreed with viewpoints being addressed. The U.S. Supreme Court upheld the constitutionality of the fairness doctrine in 1969. In *Red Lion Broadcasting v. FCC,*[114] the Court ruled that the public as well as the broadcasters had a First Amendment right to have their views expressed on the air.

The FCC's regulation of radio and television content has taken other forms as well. The FCC, for instance, prohibits the airing of indecent (offensive, but not necessarily sexual) programming, a prohibition upheld by the Supreme Court in *FCC v. Pacifica.*[115] That decision upheld an FCC fine levied on the radio broadcast of comedian George Carlin's routine about the seven words you cannot say on the air. The Court ruled that broadcasters do not have the same freedoms as their print counterparts for two reasons: broadcasting is pervasive, meaning that people can overhear a broadcast without intending to, and children can be in the audience and hear inappropriate material. This ban on indecency gained renewed attention in the early years of the twenty-first century when the FCC fined CBS the maximum $55,000 and 20 CBS-owned local stations the maximum $27,500 because of the 2004 Super Bowl halftime show in which singer Janet Jackson's nipple was briefly exposed. In a continuing crackdown, the FCC fined Clear Channel $75,000 for discussions of drug and sex on the radio program "Bubba the Love Sponge," and $1.75 million for indecency complaints against Howard Stern and other radio personalities; after this, Stern took his radio show to satellite, where he regularly criticized the FCC, which no longer had jurisdiction over his program. In what was perhaps an admission that it had gone too far in policing indecency, the FCC eventually dropped a fine against KKMG-FM radio in Colorado Springs, Colorado, which had initially been fined $7,000 in 2001 for broadcasting a song by Eminem, "The Real Slim Shady," even though the song had been edited to remove profanity and sexual language.[116]

Another form of regulation of television is self-censorship through an industry code of conduct. In 1952, the National Association of Broadcasters adopted a voluntary nationwide code banning brutality, the portrayal of kidnapping during children's programs, attacks on religion, vulgar language, illicit sex that is shown as desirable, drug use, and a variety of other activities.[117] Although the code was voluntary, stations that adhered to it were permitted to broadcast a logo that showed they were in fact adhering to the code. The idea that television programs had to be chaste is perhaps best illustrated by the attitude toward marriage and sex; because of network censors, married couples had to be shown sleeping in separate beds (as in *The Dick Van Dyke Show*), and the word *pregnancy* was banned from the air.[118]

In addition, each of the television networks employed censors whose job was to examine scripts before they were filmed (or videotaped) to eliminate anything that might be considered offensive. Sometimes the content was restricted not because of sexual or drug references but because of political commentary. The *Smothers Brothers Comedy Hour* ran into repeated problems with CBS censors in the late 1960s because of the show's criticism of the federal government and the Vietnam War; CBS canceled the show in 1969. Network censorship of content began to erode in the 1970s with the development of the late-night NBC program *Saturday Night Live*, the CBS sitcom *All in the Family* with its curmudgeonly, racist, sexist Archie Bunker, and other sitcoms with topics ranging from feminism (*Maude*) to racism (*The Jeffersons*). But perhaps no program illustrated the change in network control over content better than the ABC police drama *NYPD Blue*, which not only included nudity and frank language but was even promoted as containing such content. Donald Wildmon, leader of the conservative American Family Association, began a letter-writing campaign seeking to force ABC to cancel *NYPD Blue*.[119] Despite the outcry by Wildmon and some other conservative groups and the refusal of some stations, primarily in the South, to broadcast the program, which began airing in 1983, it became an Emmy Award–winning show.[120] In the wake of *NYPD Blue*, partial nudity, discussion of sex, homosexuality, and cursing have become commonplace in both soap operas and nighttime television. Perhaps the best illustration of how far television content has changed occurred in 2000. No longer were married couples required to sleep in separate beds;

in an episode of the sitcom *Will and Grace,* two male gay characters kissed on screen while standing in front of the *NBC Today* show set window, as a protest over the lack of kissing gay couples on television.[121]

An attempt to limit younger viewers' exposure to sexual or violent television began in 1975, when the three major networks—CBS, NBC, and ABC—agreed to a plan in which the National Association of Broadcasters Code would be amended to require a "family viewing hour" from 7 P.M. to 9 P.M. in the eastern time zone (and similar hours in other time zones). This family viewing hour was a response to complaints from the FCC and Congress that the content of television programming had become too violent and contained too many sexual images.[122] The existence of the family viewing hour was challenged in federal court by a group of television writers who alleged that it was government censorship, rather than an industry-generated initiative to curb sex and violence. In 1976, U.S. District Judge Warren J. Ferguson sided with the writers, ruling that the family viewing hour was created under pressure from the FCC and thus violated the First Amendment.[123]

In 2000, another semivoluntary regulatory system began: all new televisions with a screen 13 inches or larger had to contain a V-chip that allowed parents to limit what programs could be watched. The networks were to code all programs, much in the same way that the MPAA codes movies based on content. In addition, cable-television and satellite systems have developed programs to allow parents to limit what channels are available for viewing.

More recent attempts by the federal government to regulate television have focused on the depiction of violence. The FCC in 2007 issued a report on violent television and ts impact on children, which argued that the Supreme Court's ruling in *FCC v. Pacifica,* allowing the FCC to regulate indecency on the air, could be extended to allow Congress to pass legislation restricting violent programming.[124] No congressional action on this idea has been taken yet.

Cable and satellite programming presents a unique challenge. On the one hand, no one can be exposed to cable or satellite programming without seeking it and paying for it. On the other hand, cable and satellite services are ubiquitous in American homes. One effort to limit programming on a pay-cable channel was shot down by the U.S. Supreme Court in *U.S. v. Playboy Entertainment Group* in 2000.[125] In that case, Congress had enacted, as part of the 1996 Telecommunications Act, a requirement that sexually oriented cable channels either be blocked entirely during the hours children could be in the audience or totally scrambled. Total scrambling is a problem in many cable systems, where even a channel that is scrambled can be seen in faint images through the process called "bleed through." Playboy Entertainment, which provides the pay Playboy channel, challenged this requirement, arguing that requiring cable systems to block the channel for 16 hours a day violated the First Amendment; the Court agreed, writing that alternative methods exist for parents, including set-top blocking equipment.

VIDEO GAMES

Just as the federal government has attempted to limit the exposure of children to sexual or violent programming on television, several attempts have been made to regulate violent or sexual content of video games, both in the arcades and on home gaming systems, often on a state-by-state or city-by-city basis. Those who advocate laws prohibiting the sale of violent video games to minors argue that they are protecting immature players from the harmful effects of violent images, which could make the young players themselves more violent. Critics of these laws point to the absence of firm scientific evidence showing a link between violent content of video games and the behavior of players. So far, the courts have agreed with the critics. The Michigan legislature's 2005 attempt to block the sale of violent or sexual video games to those under the age of 17 was struck down in U.S. district court. In 2001, the City of Indianapolis failed in its attempt to permit only adults to purchase violent video games.[126] Similar efforts by the County of St. Louis, Missouri, failed in 2003,[127] as did efforts to ban the sale of violent video games in Michigan,[128] California,[129] and other states. The judges in these cases found that video games have creative graphics, story lines, music, and characters, so that they are protected by the First Amendment in the same way that movies and television programs are.

CONCLUSION

Steven Durbin, in his book *Arresting Images: Impolitic Art and Uncivil Actions,* argues that although art is sometimes shocking, it mirrors society and societal values, either soothing or provoking the viewer.[130] Whether visual art, motion pictures, theater, music, the broadcast media, or even video games, nothing pleases everyone. In addition, our notion of what constitutes art continues to evolve, from classical painting and sculpture early in the country's history to performance art and postmodern painting and sculpture today. There will always be those like Senator Helms who argue that art to which they object "leads to an erosion of civil comity and domestic tolerance within a society."[131] But rather than appreciation of the differences that make us unique human beings, those who attempt to censor artistic expression are often motivated by an emotion most of us also experience—fear. Fear of the unknown or discomfort can be powerful motivators. What will young players take away after playing a violent video game such as the Grand Theft Auto series? How will public morals be affected by a photography exhibit that includes homoerotic images? Will the audience become wanton after watching a play about incest?

Most cutting-edge artistic endeavors, those that most often attract the attention of censors, are provocative. They are meant to be. When what Kammen calls "visionary innovation in the arts"[132] encounters resistance from those in power, the outcome is often an attempt to silence that innovation. Whether the public is ever served by limiting public exposure to controversial artistic endeavors is a matter that will be debated as long as we have breath to debate. What is undebatable, though, is the fact, so obviously recounted in this chapter, that today's censored art is tomorrow's popular success.

NOTES

1. *Mutual Film Corp. v. Industrial Commission of Ohio*, 236 U.S. 230 (1915); and *Mutual Film Co. v. Hodges*, 236 U.S. 248 (1915).

2. John Houchin, *Censorship of the American Theatre in the Twentieth Century* (Cambridge: Cambridge University Press, 2003). Houchin gives a thorough history of colonial censorship of theater on pages 6–39.

3. Gregory D. Black, *Hollywood Censored: Morality Codes, Catholics and the Movies* (Cambridge: Cambridge University Press, 1994), 6.

4. James M. Skinner, *The Cross and the Cinema: The Legion of Decency and the National Catholic Office for Motion Pictures, 1933–1970* (Westport, CT: Praeger, 1993), 2–3.

5. The free speech section of the Ohio Constitution that was cited in the Court's decision read: "Every citizen may freely speak, write, and publish his sentiments on all subjects, being responsible for the abuse of the right; and no law shall be passed to restrain or abridge the liberty of speech, or of the press. In all criminal prosecutions for libel, the truth may be given in evidence to the jury, and if it shall appear to the jury that the matter charged as libelous is true, and was published with good motives, and for justifiable ends, the party shall be acquitted."

6. *Mutual Film Corp*, 236 U.S. 230 (1915).

7. It was not until 10 years later, in *Gitlow v. New York*, 268 U.S. 652 (1925), that the Supreme Court ruled that the First Amendment applied not only to the federal government but to all state and local governments through the 14th Amendment, given that amendment's guarantee that all rights protected by the U.S. Constitution could not be abridged by the states. The 14th Amendment was adopted in 1868, primarily to guarantee full citizenship rights to former slaves following the Civil War.

8. *Mutual Film Co.*, 236 U.S. The tax was $2 per film per theater, which generated $3,000 a day for the state treasury.

9. Ibid. at 257.

10. Ibid. at 258.

11. Black, *Hollywood Censored,* 13.

12. Ibid., 14.

13. Skinner, *The Cross and the Cinema,* 16.

14. It was commonly believed that Arbuckle's weight, combined with his sexual preferences, actually killed the woman.

15. Black, *Hollywood Censored,* 31. Pickford married Douglas Fairbanks.

16. Ibid., 31.

17. Ibid., 33.

18. Skinner, *The Cross and the Cinema,* 11.

19. Gerald Gardner, *The Censorship Papers: Movie Censorship Letters from the Hays Office, 1934 to 1968* (New York: Dodd, Mead & Co., 1987), xxii.

20. Ibid., xxiii.

21. Skinner, *The Cross and the Cinema,* 34.

22. Ibid.

23. Black, *Hollywood Censored,* 1.

24. Ibid., 2.

25. Black, *Hollywood Censored,* 1.

26. Michael Kelley, "Banned in Memphis: City Has High Profile in Obscenity Case," *The Commercial Appeal,* June 1, 1995.

27. *United Artists Corporation et al. v. Board of Censors of City of Memphis et al.,* 189 Tenn. 397 Tenn. Sup. Ct. 1949) at 401.

28. Ibid.

29. 334 U.S. 131 (1948).

30. 343 U.S. 495 (1952).

31. Ibid. at 501.

32. Black, *Hollywood Censored,* 229–33.

33. Ibid., 232.

34. Skinner, *The Cross and the Cinema,* 172.

35. Houchin, *Censorship of American Theatre,* 7.

36. Abe Laufe, *The Wicked Stage: A History of Theater Censorship and Harassment in the United States* (New York: Frederick Ungar, 1978), 3.

37. Ibid., 5.

38. Ibid., 8.

39. Ibid., 9.

40. Ibid., 12.

41. Ibid., 16.

42. Houchin, *Censorship of American Theatre,* 30.

43. Laufe, *Wicked Stage,* 24–25.

44. Ibid., 45.

45. Ibid., 52–53.

46. Ibid., 54–55.

47. Dawn B. Sova, *Banned Plays: Censorship History of 125 Stage Dramas* (New York: Facts on File, 2004), 250–54.

48. Laufe, *Wicked Stage,* 62–71.

49. Ibid., 73.

50. Sova, *Banned Plays,* 63–65.

51. Laufe, *Wicked Stage,* 111–14.

52. Sova, *Banned Plays,* 287–88. The same play prompted parents in Miami High School in Oklahoma to object to a *Best American Plays* book that included the drama; the book for a time was taken off the school's library shelves and placed on reserve.

53. Ibid., 106–8.

54. 420 U.S. 546 (1975) at 557–58.

55. Steven C. Dubin, *Arresting Images: Impolitic Art and Uncivil Actions* (New York: Routledge, 1992), 182.

56. Sova, *Banned Plays,* 12–14. The Supreme Court's rulings on obscenity are discussed more fully in chapter 5.

57. Laufe, *Wicked Stage,* 160.

58. Ibid., xi–xii.

59. Ibid., 23.

60. David A. Noebel, *The Marxist Minstrels: A Handbook of Communist Subversion of Music* (Tulsa, OK: American Christian College Press, 1974), 243.

61. Sony Hocklander, "Professor Leaves Evangel University after 'Full Monty' Role," *Springfield News-Leader,* September 26, 2006.

62. Jane Clapp, *Art Censorship: A Chronology of Proscribed and Prescribed Art* (Metuchen, NJ: Scarecrow Press, 1972), 15.

63. Ibid., 96–97.

64. Ibid., 113.

65. *Commonwealth of Pennsylvania v. Sharpless,* 2 Serg. & R. 91 (Pa. Sup. Ct. 1815).

66. Clapp, *Art Censorship,* 130.

67. Ibid., 140.

68. Comstock and the development of the Comstock Act are described more fully in chapter 5.

69. Clapp, *Art Censorship,* 157.

70. Russell Lynes, *The Tastemakers* (New York: Harper and Brothers, 1954), 151–52.

71. Clapp, *Art Censorship,* 163.

72. Heywod Broun and Margaret Leech, *Anthony Comstock, Roundsman of the Lord* (New York: Literary Guild of America, 1927), 216–19.

73. Clapp, *Art Censorship,* 221.

74. Michael Kammen, *Visual Shock: A History of Art Controversies in American Culture* (New York: Alfred A. Knopf, 2006), 66.

75. Lili Corbus Bezner, *Photography and Politics in America: From the New Deal into the Cold War* (Baltimore: Johns Hopkins University Press, 1999), 39–40.

76. Kammen, *Visual Shock,* 154–55.

77. Clapp, *Art Censorship,* 160–61.

78. Ibid., 280.

79. Moshe Carmilly-Weinberger, *Fear of Art: Censorship and Freedom of Expression in Art* (New York: R. R. Bowker, 1986), 155–56.

80. Clapp, *Art Censorship,* 337.

81. Ibid., 335.

82. Ibid., 397.

83. W.J.T. Mitchell, "The Violence of Public Art: Do the Right Thing," in *Art and the Public Sphere,* ed. W.J.T. Mitchell (Chicago: University of Chicago Press, 1992), 32.

84. Dubin, *Arresting Images,* 96–101.

85. Jesse Helms, *Here's Where I Stand* (New York: Random House, 2005), 140.

86. Dubin, 181–93. Because Mapplethorpe's photos had artistic value, they were not obscene under the U.S. Supreme Court's 1973 *Miller v. California* ruling that defined obscenity.

87. Ibid., 314.

88. *NEA v. Finley,* 524 U.S. 569 (1992).

89. Kammen, *Visual Shock,* 293–96.

90. Tipper Gore, "Rock Music Should Be Labeled," in *Culture Wars: Opposing Viewpoints,* ed. Fred Whitehead (San Diego: Greenhaven Press, 1984), 185–93.

91. Ibid., 190.

92. Richard Harrington, "The Capitol Hill Rock War; Emotions Run High as Musicians Confront Parents' Group at Hearing," *Washington Post,* September 20, 1985.

93. Ibid.

94. Julia Malone, "Antipornography Group Turns Senate Ear to Lurid Rock Lyrics," *Christian Science Monitor,* September 23, 1985, 24.

95. Ibid.

96. John Orman, *The Politics of Rock Music* (Chicago: Nelson-Hall, 1984), 1.

97. Noebel, *Marxist Minstrels,* i.

98. Mikal Gilmore, *Night Beat: A Shadow History of Rock and Roll* (New York: Doubleday, 1998), 23.

99. Orman, *Politics of Rock Music,* 4.

100. Ibid.

101. Ian Ingles, "The *Ed Sullivan Show* and the (Censored) Sounds of the Sixties," *Journal of Popular Culture* 39, no. 4 (2006): 558–74.

102. Ibid., 559–62.

103. Orman, *Politics of Rock Music,* 143–48.

104. Ibid., 7–8.

105. Deborah Cazan, "Concerts: Rated or Raided?: First Amendment Implications of Concert-Rating," *Vanderbilt Journal of Entertainment and Law Practice* 2 (Spring 2000): 170–83.

106. Orman, *Politics of Rock Music,* 11–13.

107. Mark A. Fox, "Market Power in Music Retailing: The Case of Wal-Mart," *Popular Music and Society* 28, no. 4 (2005): 507–19, 509.

108. Kenneth Paulson, "Regulation through Intimidation: Congressional Hearings and Political Pressure on America's Entertainment Media," *Vanderbilt Journal of Entertainment and Law Practice* 7 (Winter 2004): 78.

109. Fox, "Market Power," 509.

110. C. Hay, "Sex, Guns and Videotape: Music-Video Outlets Clean Up the Acts, Establishing Stricter Guidelines about What Can Be Aired," *Billboard,* December 1999, 40.

111. Marjorie Heins, *Sex, Sin and Blasphemy: A Guide to America's Censorship Wars* (New York: New Press, 1993), 77.

112. Ibid., 90.

113. Robert W. Haney, *Comstockery in America: Patterns of Censorship and Control* (Boston: Beacon Press, 1960), 141–42.

114. 395 U.S. 367 (1969).

115. 438 U.S. 726 (1978). The Supreme Court made a distinction between indecent (offensive) material and obscenity, which must meet a three-part test outlined in chapter 5 of this book.

116. "FCC Drops Fine over Eminem Song," Associated Press, January 9, 2002 (accessed November 3, 2007, at www.freedomforum.org).

117. Haney, *Comstockery in America,* 159–60.

118. Louis Chunovic, *One Foot on the Floor: The Curious Evolution of Sex on Television from* I Love Lucy *to* South Park (New York: TV Books, 2000), 19.

119. Sara Diamond, *Not by Politics Alone: The Enduring Influence of the Christian Right* (New York: Guilford Press, 1998), 191.

120. Ibid., 145–47.

121. Ibid., 23.

122. Geoffrey Cowan, *See No Evil: The Backstage Battle over Sex and Violence on Television* (New York: Simon and Schuster, 1979), 20.

123. *Writers Guild of America W., Inc. v. FCC,* 423 F. Supp. 1064, 1161 (C.D. Cal. 1976). Cowan, who served as a legal consultant to the Writers Guild, extensively discusses the development of and fight over the family viewing hour in his book *See No Evil* (see note 122).

124. *In the Matter of Violent Television Programming and Its Impact on Children,* FCC 07–50, 22 FCCR 7929, MB 04–261, April 25, 2007.

125. 589 U.S. 803 (2000).

126. *AAMA v. Kendrick,* 244 F.3d 572 (7th Cir. 2001).

127. *ISDA v. St. Louis County, Mo.,* 329 F.3d 954 (8th Cir. 2003).

128. *ESA v. Granholm,* 426 F. Supp. 2d 646 (E.D. Mich. 2006).

129. *Video Software Dealers Ass'n v. Schwarzenegger,* 401 F. Supp. 2d 1034 (N.D. Cal. 2005).

130. Dubin, *Arresting Images,* 1.

131. Helms, *Here's Where I Stand,* 142.

132. Kammen, *Visual Shock,* 384.

5

Censorship and Sexually Explicit Material

The depiction of sexual activity is not unique to our nation or our time. Illustrations and writings about sex are almost as old as recorded history. Greek and Roman drama and poetry contained enough sexual material to make a sensitive person blush,[1] drawings depicting intercourse were found on the walls of a brothel in Pompeii,[2] and even Greek pottery depicted scenes of orgies, prostitution, and homosexuality.[3]

The first conviction for obscenity in the United States occurred in 1815, when a Pennsylvania judge ruled that Jesse Sharpless had attempted to "debauch and corrupt, and to raise and create in (youths') minds inordinate and lustful desires," also ruling that if the works Sharpless displayed corrupted just one person, the entire work was obscene.[4] For almost the next 200 years, the question of what makes something obscene has plagued the court system in this country.

In the United States, discussions, government reports, and court cases about sexually explicit material could fill volumes of printed material. Some would argue that trying to prevent the manufacture or distribution of sexually explicit material denies the Miltonian "marketplace of ideas" approach to the First Amendment by preventing people from reading or seeing what they want, that is, the idea that "all censorship contradicts freedom" because "a free society is based on the principle that each individual has the right to decide what art or entertainment she wants to receive."[5] Others would argue that the sex industry is a billion-dollar-plus industry that exploits women and children and cheapens the intrinsic humanness of love. Sex, writes Irving

Kristol, "is an act both animal and human. But when sex is public, the viewer does not see—cannot see—the sentiments and ideals. He can only see the animal coupling."[6]

HISTORY OF OBSCENITY REGULATION

The idea that the government should regulate sexually explicit material is not new; when the founders of the United States created our form of government, they adopted many of the laws and policies that had been in effect in England, one of which officially condemned the depiction of sex in anyform.

English common law making it a crime to distribute filthy or obscene material began developing before the United States won its War of Independence, but few laws specifically outlawed obscenity. With the beginning of the Victorian Age in the 1800s, however, governments began to enact laws that banned depiction of sex or even hinted at sex.[7] The first English law banning obscenity was the Obscene Publications Act of 1857, which allowed constables and police to enter homes or businesses to seize obscene material.[8] One of the earliest cases under this law was the case of *Regina v. Hicklin* in 1868,[9] in which the defendant, Henry Scott, was accused of violating the law by possessing 252 copies of a pamphlet concerning Catholic priests and inappropriate questions asked of women during confessionals.[10] Scott lost at trial when Justice Benjamin Hicklin ruled that the pamphlet was obscene. Scott won on appeal; however, the government then appealed that decision, and the Court of the Queen's Bench ruled once again that the pamphlet was obscene.[11] Justice James Edward Cockburn, joined by two other justices, ruled that an isolated section of a work (such as a book) could be taken out of context, and if that section would tend to corrupt the most susceptible person in the society, then the work as a whole was obscene and could be banned. In his decision, Cockburn wrote, "I think the best test of obscenity is this, whether the tendency of the matter charged as obscene is to deprave and corrupt those whose minds are open to such immoral influences, and into whose hands a publication of this sort may fall."[12] The practical effect of this ruling was to make anything with sexual or other offensive content illegal under English law. The effect this English case had on the United States was far-reaching, being adopted by the courts in this country and making many classic works obscene. As an example, the decision of a U.S. district court in the 1883 case of *U.S. v. Britton* demonstrates that the *Hicklin* rule was alive and well in America: "It is not a question of whether it would corrupt the morals of every person. It is illegal if it would suggest impure and libidinous thoughts in the minds of the young and inexperienced."[13] The U.S. Congress enacted its first antiobscenity laws in 1842, banning the importation of obscenity into the United States.[14] The transmission of obscene material through the mail was banned in 1857.[15]

This era of increased attention to regulation of sexually explicit material brought America one of its more notable censors, Anthony Comstock, a New York grocer who crusaded against the sale and consumption of indecent material, which, in the words of one biographer, was sold on the streets of New York "as freely as roasted chestnuts."[16] Reading one of these licentious publications, Comstock wrote, "breeds lust. Lust defiles the body, debauches the imagination, corrupts the mind, deadens the will, destroys the memory, scars the conscience, hardens the heart, and damns the soul."[17] Comstock put his words into action by helping to create the New York Society for the Suppression of Vice in 1873. This group set out to eradicate sex from all publicly available material; it did not matter to Comstock whether the material had any artistic merit.[18]

Congress had already passed an antiobscenity law by 1865, prohibiting the mailing of any obscene material. But that law was not enough for Comstock, who began lobbying Congress for a tougher antipornography law. Congress responded by passing, after less than an hour of debate, a law that became known as the Comstock Act, which gave the U.S. post office the power to prohibit the mailing of anything that was deemed to be lewd, indecent, filthy, or obscene.[19] Given its new power, the post office was in the market for a chief censor, and Comstock was in the market for a job that would help him to eradicate material that inflamed the secret desires of the unsuspecting. It was a perfect match. He was hired as a special agent of the post office.[20]

In his new job as America's chief censor, Comstock went at his task with vigor. Shortly before his death in 1915, he bragged that he had "convicted enough to fill a passenger train of sixty coaches containing sixty passengers each and the sixty-first almost full. I have destroyed 160 tons of obscene literature."[21] Despite his self-promotion, Comstock was not universally admired. In one notable incident, Comstock spotted a display in a New York candy maker's window that was a reproduction of Hans Makart's "The Triumph of Charles the Fifth," in which horses are led by nude boys as Charles rides into Antwerp. He entered the store and demanded that the storeowner remove the picture from the window; the storeowner complied. Shortly afterward, *Life* reproduced the picture the way, it wrote, Comstock would like it to appear, with the horses wearing pants.[22] In fact, Comstock was routinely ridiculed in the press with editorial cartoons, which depicted him lounging with Sappho, having cloven feet (as if he were Satan), and hauling a woman into court for giving birth to a naked baby. In one of his more noteworthy crusades, he took on the Irish playwright George Bernard Shaw, calling him a "smut peddler." Shaw responded by calling "Comstockery...the world's standing joke at the expense of the United States."[23] Despite the ridicule that Comstock suffered, the law he lobbied for created the framework for laws still existing today that ban the mailing of obscene material. Many of the issues Comstock fought over remain contentious issues today, such as the role of sex in art and the exposure of children to depictions of sex.[24]

Of course, defining what is obscene is not a simple matter. In fact, the courts throughout the first half of the twentieth century struggled to come up with a workable definition that could be applied across the board. They failed; judges, however, gradually began to acknowledge that the *Hicklin* rule, which made a work obscene if even an isolated section was potentially damaging to the most susceptible person, was unworkable as a definition of obscenity. The New York Supreme Court, ruling in 1894 that classic works by authors such as Ovid and Rabelais were not obscene, wrote that "to condemn a standard literary work, because of a few of its episodes, would compel the exclusion of a very large proportion of the works of fiction by the most famous writers of the English language."[25] Another New York court wrote that to follow the *Hicklin* rule would make works by Aristophanes and Chaucer and even the Bible obscene.[26] Other judges followed suit, most notably Judge Learned Hand in the 1913 case of *United States v. Kennerly,* when he wrote that the *Hicklin* test was outdated, noting instead that the "average conscience" was a better basis for determining obscenity.[27] In 1933 District Judge John Woolsey converted Hand's "average conscience" test to a test of whether a work was obscene in its entirety to the "average person."[28] Woolsey's decision came in a case to determine whether the James Joyce novel *Ulysses* was obscene because a small section contained a discussion of sexual behavior. On appeal, Woolsey's decision was upheld by the court of appeals. Judges Learned Hand and Augustus Hand believed that the *Hicklin* test, which gauged obscenity based on the effect of an isolated section of a work on the most susceptible person in society, was not a good measure; instead, they wrote, "the question ... is whether a publication taken as a whole has a libidinous effect."[29] It would be 14 more years before the U.S. Supreme Court would tackle the question of obscenity in *Roth v. U.S.*[30]

MODERN OBSCENITY REGULATION

The *Roth* case began when Samuel Roth, a publisher and bookseller in New York, was indicted on 24 counts and convicted on 4 counts of violating federal law by mailing obscene circulars and an obscene book; the law, a slight revision of the Comstock Act 50 years earlier, prohibited mailing of "every obscene, lewd, lascivious, or filthy book, pamphlet, picture, paper, letter, writing, print, or other publication of an indecent character."[31] Roth appealed to the Supreme Court, contending that his conviction violated the First Amendment's protection of free speech, as well as the Ninth and Tenth amendments, by allowing the federal government to punish him when the states alone should prosecute obscenity. In another case at the same time, the Supreme Court was asked to overturn the obscenity conviction of David Alberts, who was convicted of violating California law by selling obscene books and preparing an obscene advertisement for those books. Alberts argued, unsuccessfully, that the California law banning material that raises "lustful thoughts" was unconstitutionally vague and also that the state should be able to ban only material that led to antisocial behavior.[32]

In its first ruling on the question of what defines obscenity, the Court expressly dismissed the *Hicklin* principle and came up with its own definition of obscenity: "whether to the average person, applying contemporary community standards, the dominant theme of the material taken as a whole appeals to prurient interest."[33] In the same decision, the Court ruled that obscenity as a category of expression is not protected by the First Amendment because it is without redeeming social virtue; it also ruled that the federal government may indeed prosecute obscenity cases.

The *Roth* test, as it became known, marked the first time the Supreme Court specified that works had to be considered in their entirety, rather than in isolated sections, when determining whether they were obscene. It also essentially ended the debate of whether obscenity is protected speech. But the *Roth* test was troublesome in that it raised almost as many questions as it answered. How does a court determine who an "average person" is? How does a judge or jury determine what "contemporary community standards" are? Within nine years of the *Roth* decision, the Court handled a series of decisions that attempted to clarify some of those questions.

The Supreme Court's first decision post-*Roth* came two years later in *Kingsley International Pictures v. the Regents of the University of the State of New York,* a case concerning the movie version of D. H. Lawrence's *Lady Chatterley's Lover.*[34] The case involved a film company's challenge of a New York state law that allowed the state board of censors, governed by the state board of regents, to refuse to permit the showing of the movie unless three scenes were excised. The company refused to remove the scenes, and the board of censors declared the entire movie immoral. The Supreme Court ruled that the state law was unconstitutional because it prohibited the movie on the grounds that it advocated an unpopular idea (that adultery might be acceptable behavior in some circumstances) and, therefore, violated the First Amendment guarantee of free speech.[35] In a concurring opinion, Justice Hugo Black cautioned his colleagues about starting down a path in which they would be reviewing and ruling on obscenity cases book by book and movie by movie, stating "my belief is that this Court is about the most inappropriate Supreme Board of Censors that could be found."[36] But that is exactly what the Court became. Bob Woodward and Scott Armstrong's behind-the-scenes book examining the Supreme Court's inner workings tells how some of the justices and their law clerks would make popcorn for "movie day," the day they watched the films that were the subject of obscenity appeals. A popular cartoon of the time showed nine men in robes (there were not yet any women on the Court) sitting in a darkened room watching a dirty movie. Justice Black's fear was coming true.

In the next few years, the Supreme Court took on nine more obscenity cases. Ironically, one concerned a book written in 1750, *Memoirs of a Woman of Pleasure* (commonly called *Fanny Hill*), that had already been ruled obscene by a Massachusetts court in 1821.[37] But before getting to the *Fanny Hill* case, the Court first had to dispose of a number of other cases. In *Smith v. California,* the Court ruled that a state, in prosecuting an obscenity case, had to prove the legal concept of *scienter,* that is, that the accused had knowledge that the material was obscene.[38] Next, in *Manual Enterprises v. Day,* the Court overturned an Alexandria, Virginia, post office ruling banning from the mails some magazines, *Manual, Trim,* and *Grecian Guild Pictorial,* that contained nude or nearly nude models, although a badly split Court could not agree why; Justice John Harlan wrote that the *Roth* test meant that material had to be "patently offensive" to be obscene.[39]

Two years later, the Supreme Court issued a ruling in *Jacobellis v. Ohio* that is notable mainly because of a phrase in a concurring opinion that illustrates how confusing the *Roth* rule had become.[40] The case involved a movie, *Les Amants* (translated into English as *The Lovers*), that was found to have violated Ohio antiobscenity law because of a graphic love scene near the end of the film. Nico Jacobellis was found guilty of possessing obscenity and exhibiting obscenity by showing the film. The Court, in its opinion, acknowledged that the *Roth* test was imperfect and ruled that the movie, in part because it had been listed by several critics as one of the best movies of the year, was not obscene. In its decision, the Court noted that the justices had watched the movie before passing judgment. More noteworthy than the decision, however, was Justice Potter Stewart's concurring opinion, in which he stated clearly the confusion over the Court's definition of obscenity: "It is possible to read the Court's opinion in *Roth*...in a variety of ways.... Under the First and Fourteenth Amendments criminal laws in this area are constitutionally limited to hard-core pornography. I shall not today attempt further to define the kinds of materials I understand to be embraced within that shorthand description; and perhaps I could never succeed in intelligibly doing so. But I know it when I see it, and the motion picture involved in this case is not that."[41]

"I know it when I see it" is a difficult standard for anyone to follow in determining whether a work is obscene, and the Court continued to refine its definition. In a two-day period in December 1965, the Court heard arguments in three separate obscenity cases. The first, *Ginzburg v. U.S.,* involved Ralph Ginzburg, who had been convicted of violating federal obscenity law by publishing the magazine *Eros,* a newsletter called *Liaison,* and a book titled *The Housewife's Handbook on Selective Promiscuity.*[42] Ginzburg argued that redeeming content, in the form of worthy stories, meant that his publications were not obscene. The Court ruled that Ginzburg's publications were primarily designed to appeal to prurient interest and were therefore obscene. The second case, heard the same day as *Ginzburg,* was *Mishkin v. N.Y.,* which concerned books that dealt with sadomasochism, homosexuality, and fetishism.[43] Mishkin argued that his books would not likely appeal to the prurient interest of the "average person" specified in *Roth.* But the Court ruled that the books were obscene because of their appeal to the targeted audience. The third case, mentioned earlier, concerned a Massachusetts ruling that John Cleland's 1750 book known as *Fanny Hill* was obscene under state law.[44] Arguments before the Court focused on the literary worth of the book, and the Court ruled that even if sex was a dominant theme, the book would have to be "utterly without redeeming value" to be banned; since there was no doubt that *Fanny Hill* was a literary work, it was not obscene.

Two years later, the Court began to refine further its concept of obscenity, creating categories of unprotected expression based on the audience. In *Ginsberg v. N.Y.,* Sam Ginsberg (not to be confused with *Ginzburg v. U.S.*) was convicted of violating state law by selling sexually graphic, but not obscene, material (the Court referred to them as "girlie magazines") to minors from his Long Island luncheonette.[45] The Court ruled that the state has an interest in protecting minors from sexual content, even if that sexual content consists solely of nude photos that fall far short of the *Roth* standard.

To this point, the Supreme Court's rulings on obscenity had dealt with material that had been distributed in some manner, either through sales or through the mail. But in 1969, the Court was asked to determine whether mere possession of obscene material was subject to punishment. Federal agents, using a search warrant authorizing them to look for evidence of illegal gambling, raided the home of Georgia resident Robert Stanley. They found no evidence of bookmaking, but the agents found did find three reels of motion pictures in a desk drawer. Using a projector they found in the closet, the agents proceeded to watch the movies in Stanley's home. Subsequently, Stanley was indicted and later convicted of violating a state law prohibiting possession of obscene material. The Supreme Court, however, overturned his conviction, ruling that mere possession of obscene material in the home without any attempt to distribute or transport it was protected by the First Amendment.[46] Citing the right to privacy, which the Court first described in the 1958 case *Griswold v. Connecticut*,[47] the Court noted the problem of how an individual could possess obscene material in the home without purchasing or transporting it, actions that would not be protected by the First Amendment. But the Court said authorities could not bypass constitutional problems by simply assuming that Stanley had violated the law.

The Supreme Court's case-by-case review of obscenity cases, its transformation into a "Supreme Court of Censorship," highlighted one of the problems of the *Roth* standard; while trying to define obscenity, the Court had created as many questions as it answered. The justices attempted to remedy this problem in *Miller v. California,* the first major obscenity case since a change in the court's membership moved it in a more conservative direction: two liberal justices stepped down (Chief Justice Earl Warren in 1969 and Justice Hugo Black in 1971), and President Nixon replaced them with conservative Chief Justice Warren Burger and Justice (later Chief Justice) William Rehnquist.[48] The *Miller* case began when Marvin Miller was charged with violating California obscenity law by mailing "adult" brochures advertising four books he was selling: *Intercourse, Man-Woman, Sex Orgies Illustrated,* and *An Illustrated History of Pornography,* as well as the film *Marital Intercourse.* In upholding Miller's conviction, five justices (a bare majority) modified the *Roth* test by developing a new three-part test for obscenity. The first part of the *Miller* test, echoing the *Roth* test, is "whether the average person, applying contemporary community standards, would find that the work, taken as a whole, appeals to the prurient interest." The second part of the *Miller* test is "whether the work depicts or describes, in a patently offensive way, sexual conduct specifically defined by applicable state law. The third part was "whether the work, taken as a whole, lacks serious literary, artistic, political or scientific value" (this part has become known as the SLAP test, if the categories are rearranged slightly).[49]

It is difficult to overstate the importance of the *Miller* decision. With its three-part test, the justices devised a system for punishing obscenity but still allowing sexual content that has merit as art, science, literature, or political commentary. That part of the *Miller* test prevents prosecution for displaying material that is objectionable to some but still has value to others. The new test for obscenity also specifically stated that obscenity had to depict sexual conduct in a patently offensive way, not merely in a manner that was morally offensive. The *Miller* test still stands as the official U.S. policy on the difference between obscenity and protected expression. That does not mean, however, that the Supreme Court has not continued to hear obscenity cases.

In the same year as *Miller,* the Supreme Court was asked again to consider whether watching a sexually explicit motion picture violated obscenity law.

The Court had ruled in *Stanley v. Georgia* that the First Amendment protected mere possession of such a film in the home, but a majority of the justices reached a different conclusion about showing a sexually explicit movie in a theater. In *Paris Adult Theatre I v. Slaton,* the Court ruled against two Atlanta, Georgia, movie theaters and their owners, who were accused of violating Georgia law by showing patrons two films, *Magic Mirror* and *It All Comes Out in the End.*[50] The movie theater owners argued that only consenting adults who paid an admission fee could see the films, and a sign on the door read, "Adult Theatre—you must be 21 and able to prove it." The Court ruled that the Georgia legislature had the right to ban the showing of obscene films because it could assume a link between adult films and sex crimes, even though the Supreme Court acknowledged no scientific evidence proving that link.

As stated earlier, the Supreme Court in the *Ginsberg* decision ruled that states can prohibit the distribution of sexual material to minors, even if the material falls short of obscenity. But what about pornography that is made using minors? In a pair of cases, the Supreme Court upheld the government's power to outlaw the production or possession of what became known as "kiddie porn." In the first case, the Supreme Court upheld the conviction of Paul Ferber, who had been convicted of two counts of violating a New York State law by selling an undercover officer two films that consisted almost entirely of young boys masturbating.[51] In its decision, the Court dismissed the defendant's claim that a law banning sexually explicit but not obscene material violated the First Amendment's guarantee of free speech. Rather, the Court wrote that the production and distribution of sexual material involving minors are intrinsically related to the abuse of minors, and the government has a duty to protect children from sexual abuse. Seven years later, the Court went further by permitting the government to outlaw even the possession of kiddie porn.[52]

The Supreme Court also has given its approval to city efforts to limit the location of adult theaters and other adult establishments in a pair of decisions, *Young v. American Mini Theaters*[53] and *Renton v. Playtime Theater,*[54] allowing communities to enact zoning restrictions on such businesses, as long as the zoning is not a complete ban. In the *Renton* case, for instance, the city of Renton, Washington, was upheld in its zoning rules limiting the establishment of adult movie theaters within 1,000 feet of residences, apartment buildings, churches, schools, and other similar institutions.

In 1978, the Supreme Court created another category of expression not protected by the First Amendment. *FCC v. Pacifica* involved a challenge of the Federal Communications Commission (FCC) rules, which had been in effect since Congress enacted the Federal Radio Act in 1927, giving the federal government authority to regulate broadcasting and banning obscenity and indecency over the air.[55] A station owned by Pacifica broadcast a recording of comedian George Carlin about the "seven words you can't say on the air." The FCC, reacting to a complaint from a listener, fined Pacifica for airing indecent programming. Pacifica appealed, arguing that speech falling short of obscenity is protected by the First Amendment. The Court, however, said speech does not have to be obscene to be banned from the airwaves; it simply must be offensive, even if it doesn't appeal to prurient interest. The Court gave two rationales: first, broadcasting is pervasive, and people can be unintentionally exposed to programming merely by overhearing someone else's radio, and, second, children can be in the audience, and the government has an obligation to protect children from indecency.[56]

An attempt to expand the indecency standard to the Internet, however, failed in *Reno v. ACLU.*[57] Congress had enacted, and President Clinton signed into law, the Communication Decency Act of 1996, which made it a crime, punishable by up to two years in prison and $250,000 in fines, to post Internet material that was "indecent" or "patently offensive" if that material could be viewed by a minor. The Supreme Court, however, upheld a lower-court injunction preventing the law from taking effect because it criminalized constitutionally protected expression.

Congress reacted to the *Reno v. ACLU* decision by enacting another law, the Child Online Protection Act of 1998, also known as COPA. It would criminalize, with punishments of up to six months in jail and a $50,000 fine, commercial material on the Web that fails a modification of the *Miller* test: "(A) the average person, applying contemporary community standards, would find, taking the material as a whole and with respect to minors, is designed to appeal to, or is designed to pander to, the prurient interest; (B) depicts, describes, or represents, in a manner patently offensive with respect to minors, an actual or simulated sexual act or sexual contact, an actual or simulated normal or perverted sexual act, or a lewd exhibition of the genitals or post-pubescent female breast; and (C) taken as a whole, lacks serious literary, artistic, political, or scientific value for minors."[58] That law was also challenged as an infringement of the First Amendment, but the Supreme Court did allow one part of the law to take effect, requiring any school or library that receives federal funds (almost all do) to install filters on their publicly accessible computer terminals, blocking indecent material.[59]

PROBLEMS IN DEFINING OBSCENITY

Several cases highlight the problems some prosecutors, judges, and other officials have in interpreting the *Miller* standard. The first occurred in Indianapolis, when the city council attempted to outlaw pornography because it is an assault on women. The council was reacting to publications by two women, Andrea Dworkin and Catherine MacKinnon, who argued that sexual material subjugates women by making them objects for domination and conquest by men. The council then passed an ordinance allowing anyone to file a civil suit against the producer or distributor of pornography in which

(1) Women are presented as sexual objects who enjoy pain or humiliation; or (2) Women are presented as sexual objects who experience sexual pleasure in being raped; or (3) Women are presented as sexual objects tied up or cut up or mutilated or bruised or physically hurt, or as dismembered or truncated or fragmented or severed into body parts; or (4) Women are presented as being penetrated by objects or animals; or (5) Women are presented in scenarios of degradation, injury, abasement, torture, shown as filthy or inferior, bleeding, bruised, or hurt in a context that makes these conditions sexual; or (6) Women are presented as sexual objects for domination, conquest, violation, exploitation, possession, or use, or through postures or positions of servility or submission or display.[60]

The ordinance, which could essentially outlaw nonobscene material, was challenged in federal court, and both the U.S. district court and the Seventh Circuit Court of Appeals ruled that the ordinance violated the First Amendment because it did not follow the *Miller* standard at all, making no mention of material appealing to prurient interest, of sexual conduct, or of the SLAP test.

Four years later, a pair of cases brought even more attention to the limits *Miller* places on restrictions on expression. In the first case, a Broward County, Florida, sheriff's deputy, after listening to several songs on the rap group 2 Live Crew's recording *As Nasty As They Wanna Be,* asked a county judge to declare the recording obscene; when the judge agreed, area music stores were told to remove the recording from sale. Luther Campbell, a member of the group, sued in U.S. district court, but Judge Jose Gonzales Jr. ruled that the recording was obscene because it referred to male and female genitalia, oral and group sex, and other sexual behaviors.[61] Gonzales's decision was appealed, and the 11th Circuit Court of Appeals overturned Gonzales's decision, ruling that the recording did not meet the *Miller* standard because, as rap music commenting on social issues, it had serious artistic value.[62]

The second case involved the noted photographer Robert Mapplethorpe and an attempt by the Cincinnati, Ohio, prosecutor to punish a museum director for obscenity. A Hamilton County grand jury, at the request of the county prosecutor, indicted the Contemporary Arts Center and its director, Dennis Barrie, on charges of pandering obscenity because of nudity and homoerotic photographs and use of a minor in producing nudity because of two photographs that had children in poses. A U.S. district judge, however, prohibited local officials from interfering with the 170-photo exhibit, and a Hamilton County jury acquitted the museum and its director after a trial.[63]

Several other photographers ran afoul of obscenity law for taking photos of nude children. Grandmother Maria Rubin was arrested in 2000 in Upper Montclair, New Jersey, booked, and released on $50,000 bond when she dropped off at a fast photo-development booth film that showed her three- and eight-year-old granddaughters frolicking in a bedroom before they took a bath; the case was dismissed when she completed a pretrial intervention program for first-time offenders.[64]

ARGUMENTS FOR CENSORSHIP

A number of groups, including the Christian Coalition, the American Family Association, the Concerned Women for America, the Eagle Forum, and Focus on the Family, as well as innumerable local groups, have been trying for years to eliminate gratuitous sex from the entertainment industry.[65] They have fought to eliminate pornography on the Internet and to limit juveniles' access to books containing sexually explicit passages, and they have boycotted movies depicting what they see as questionable morality.

Among those who favor restrictions are Christian conservatives who see a link between exposure to pornography and crimes such as rape and child murder. John Hughes, writing in the *Christian Science Monitor,* blamed pornography exposure for the case of a 20-year-old charged with murder and child kidnapping: "It should not require a doctorate in psychology to understand that what we see and hear can influence our behavior."[66] Paul Blankenship, a student at Vanguard University in California, created a student-run organization, Erase the Dark, to promote awareness of the dangers of pornography, which, he says, creates child molesters and rapists.[67] Mark Galli, senior managing editor of *Christianity Today,* complained of the widespread availability of sexually explicit material on the Internet: "Porn's pervasiveness on the Internet has, for example, normalized it for many. Playboy and Penthouse now seem downright wholesome in comparison. Cable companies like AT&T offer premium porn channels as if they were just another ESPN."[68]

Other opponents of sexually explicit material oppose it because of its degrading effect on both consumers and those who are exploited by pornography producers. Conservative author Irving Kristol, for instance, writes that pornography's "whole purpose is to treat people obscenely, to deprive human beings of their specifically human dimension."[69]

Others view pornography as inherently demeaning to women, who are most often depicted in such materials. One writer who urges restrictions on pornography is feminist Catherine MacKinnon, who views pornography as part of the larger problem of sexual harassment, prostitution, and subjugation of women: "Women in pornography are bound, battered, tortured, harassed, raped, and sometimes killed; or in the glossy men's entertainment magazines, 'merely' humiliated, molested, objectified, and used.... In order to produce what the [male] consumer wants to see, it first must be done to someone, usually a woman, a woman with few real choices. Because he wants to see it done, it is done to her."[70] Similarly, Melissa Farley, a research and clinical psychologist, equates pornography with torture: "There is great silence regarding the torture of women in prostitution during the making of pornography. Yet torture is commonplace in pornography."[71]

The Attorney General's Commission on Pornography, which spent months examining the pervasiveness and effect of sexually explicit material, issued a report in 1985 stating: "We all are concerned about the impact of such materials on children, on attitudes toward women, on the relationships between the sexes, and on attitudes on sex in general."[72] The commission issued nearly 90 recommendations for ways the government could combat pornography, including a renewed effort by federal prosecutors to pursue criminal charges against those producing or selling obscenity. But developments since the commission issued its report, including the terrorist attack on the United States on September 11, 2001, have shifted prosecutors' attention from obscenity to the prevention of further terrorist attacks. U.S. Attorney General Alberto Gonzales, on taking office in 2005, announced that his administration would have a renewed focus on enforcing antiobscenity laws, but even that pledge was never fulfilled because of the effort to enforce terrorism laws.[73]

CONCLUSION

While the Supreme Court has been clear since 1957 that obscenity does not have First Amendment protection, there are three basic approaches to whether and how much sexually explicit but not obscene material should be regulated.

The first, what might be called an absolutist approach, claims that the First Amendment permits "no law restricting...freedom of speech or of the press," and that is what it means. Material that is not obscene is protected expression and should not be regulated. As Marjorie Heins writes in *Sex, Sin and Blasphemy,* "A free society is based on the principle that each individual has a right to decide what art or entertainment she wants to receive—or create.... All censorship contradicts freedom."[74]

A second approach, the moral argument, is that sexually explicit material degrades both the producers and consumers, and society suffers as a result. A third, the pornography-as-subjugation approach, argues that sexually explicit material degrades the subjects, usually women, by making them objects rather than people. MacKinnon, for instance, equates pornography with rape: "The evidence shows that the use of pornography makes it impossible for men to tell when sex is forced, that women are women, and that rape is rape. Pornography makes men hostile and aggressive toward women, and it makes women silent."[75]

Regardless of the philosophical approach, to pornography, sexually explicit material is not disappearing, despite court decisions, prosecutions, campaigns by crusaders, and government reports aimed at limiting the manufacture, distribution, or consumption of it.

NOTES

1. *Final Report of the Attorney General's Commission on Pornography* (Nashville, TN: Rutledge Hill Press, 1986), 9.

2. Ibid.

3. Sofia A. Souli, *Love Life of the Ancient Greeks* (Athens, Greece: Toubis, 1997).

4. *Commonwealth of Pennsylvania v. Sharpless,* 2 Serg. & R. 91 (Pa. Sup. Ct. 1815).

5. Marjorie Heins, *Sex, Sin and Blasphemy: A Guide to America's Censorship Wars* (New York: New Press, 1993), 6.

6. Irving Kristol, "Pornography, Obscenity and the Case for Censorship," in *The Neocon Reader,* ed. Irwin Stelzer (New York: Grove Press, 2004), 169–80, esp. 170.

7. Women at this time were expected to cover their legs, including the ankles, so that the appearance of these "private" parts would not inflame the men.

8. Haig A. Bosmajian, *Obscenity and Freedom of Expression* (New York: Burt Franklin, 1976), ii.

9. James Jackson Kilpatrick, *The Smut Peddlers* (Westport, CT: Greenwood Press, 1960), 109.

10. The title was "The Confessional Unmasked: Shewing the Depravity of the Roman Priesthood, the Iniquity of the Confessional, and the Questions Put to Females in Confession."

11. Kilpatrick, *Smut Peddlers,* 110.

12. Ibid., 111.

13. 17 Fed. 131 (1883).

14. Heywood Broun and Margaret Leech, *Anthony Comstock: Roundsman of the Lord* (New York: Literary Guild of America, 1927), 79.

15. Ibid.

16. Ibid., 78.

17. Ibid., 80.

18. *Final Report of the Attorney General's Commission,* 32.

19. Heins, *Sex, Sin and Blasphemy,* 19.

20. Ibid., 146.

21. *Final Report of the Attorney General's Commission,* 13.

22. Broun and Leech, *Anthony Comstock,* 225.

23. Ibid., 229–30.

24. Margaret A. Blanchard and John E. Semonche, "Anthony Comstock and His Adversaries: The Mixed Legacy of This Battle for Free Speech," *Communication Law and Policy* 11, no. 3 (2006): 317–66.

25. *In re Worthington,* 30 N.Y.S. 361 (1894).

26. *Halsey v. the New York Society for the Suppression of Vice,* 136 N.E. 219 (N.Y. Ct. App. 1922).

27. 209 F. 119 (1913).

28. *United States v. One Book Called "Ulysses,"* 5 F. Supp. 182 (1933 S.D. N.Y.).

29. *United States v. One Book Called "Ulysses,"* 72 F.2d 705 (1943 2nd Cir.).

30. 354 U.S. 476.

31. Ibid. at 479n1.

32. Ibid.

33. Ibid. at 489. The term *prurient* comes from the Latin word meaning to burn or itch, and in this context it means material designed to sexually arouse the consumer.

34. 360 U.S. 684 (1957).

35. Ibid.

36. Ibid. at 690.

37. *Commonwealth of Massachusetts v. Holmes,* 17 Mass. 336 (1821).

38. 361 U.S. 147 (1959).

39. 370 U.S. 478 (1962).

40. 378 U.S. 184 (1964).

41. Ibid. at 1967.

42. 383 U.S. 463 (1966).

43. 383 U.S. 502 (1996).

44. *Memoirs v. Massachusetts,* 383 U.S. 413 (1966).

45. 390 U.S. 629 (1968).

46. *Stanley v. Georgia,* 394 U.S. 557 (1869).

47. 381 U.S. 479 (1958). The Supreme Court, in ruling unconstitutional a state law prohibiting communication about birth control, cited for the first time in a majority decision that an inherent right to privacy in the Constitution, although not explicitly stated.

48. 413 U.S. 15 (1973).

49. Ibid. at 25. A later Supreme Court decision, *Pope v. Illinois,* 481 U.S. 497 (1987), clarified that the SLAP had to be serious content, not just any material that related to science, literature, art, or politics.

50. 413 U.S. 49 (1973).

51. *New York v. Ferber,* 458 U.S. 474 (1983).

52. *Osborne v. Ohio,* 495 U.S. 103 (1990).

53. 427 U.S. 50 (1976).

54. 479 U.S. 41 (1986).

55. 430 U.S. 726 (1978).

56. As an outgrowth of this case, Congress enacted the "safe harbor" law, which sets out a time when children are presumably not in the audience and slightly more mature programming can be aired, from 10 P.M. to 6 A.M.

57. 521 U.S. 844 (1997).

58. 47 U.S.C. § 231.

59. *Ashcroft v. ACLU,* 542 U.S. 656 (2004). This decision upheld a temporary injunction blocking other parts of COPA from taking effect because it violates the First Amendment. The filter law allows the filters to be overridden if requested by individual adult users.

60. *American Booksellers v. Hudnut,* 771 F.2d 323 (7th Cir. 1985) at 324.

61. *Skywalker Records v. Navarro,* 739 F. Supp. 578 (S.D. Fla. 1990).

62. *Luke Records v. Navarro,* 960 F.2d 134 (11th Cir. 1990). The name of the record company changed from when the district court heard the case. This case marked the first time a recording was the subject of an obscenity case after *Miller.*

63. "Mapplethorpe Controversy Reverberates in Cincinnati 10 Years Later," The Associated Press, April 11, 2000 (accessed November 2, 2007, at www.freedomfo rum.org).

64. Maria Rubin, Jacqueline Livingston, Marilyn Zimmerman, and Betsy Schneider, "'Not a Pretty Picture': Four Photographers Tell Their Personal Stories about Child 'Pornography' and Censorship," in *Censoring Culture: Contemporary Threats to Free Expression,* ed. Robert Atkins and Svetlana Mintcheva (New York: New Press, 2006), 213–27.

65. Sara Diamond, *Not by Politics Alone: The Enduring Influence of the Christian Right* (New York: Guilford Press, 1998), 189.

66. John Hughes, "Pornography: The Social Ill behind Some Dangerous Crimes," *Christian Science Monitor,* August 16, 2006, 9.

67. Kate Schmetzer, "Fighting Porn," *Campus Life,* December 2005, 30.

68. Mark Galli, "Infection in the Body," *Christianity Today* 45, no. 4 (2001): 8.

69. Kristol, "Pornography, Obscenity and Censorship," 171.

70. Catherine MacKinnon, "Pornography as Defamation and Discrimination," *Boston University Law Review* 71 (1991): 793–815, esp. 796–97.

71. Melissa Farley, "Sex for Sale: Prostitution, Trafficking, and Cultural Amnesia: What We Must Not Know to Keep the Business of Sexual Exploitation Running Smoothly," *Yale Journal of Law and Feminism* 18 (2006): 109–44, esp. 123.

72. *Final Report of the Attorney General's Commission,* 47.

73. Eric Lichtblau, "Gonzales Lays Out His Priorities at Justice Dept," *New York Times,* March 1, 2005.

74. Heins, *Sex, Sin and Blasphemy,* 6.

75. MacKinnon, "Pornography," 800.

6

Regulation of Student Expression

When students enter a public high school or college, they have certain expectations and must meet certain demands. On the one hand, students in both settings are learning how to express themselves in a way that allows them to reach their full potential as citizens; inherent in that burgeoning citizenship is the freedom to state opinions that might be counter to accepted viewpoints. On the other hand, students are in school ostensibly to learn, and school officials have the obligation to provide an environment free from any distraction that might hinder learning. Those two goals—freedom of expression and freedom to learn—often collide.

The idea that students, whether in primary or secondary schools or in colleges and universities, have the right to free speech is a relatively recent development, compared to the long history of freedom of expression in this country. In fact, students' free expression rights, which reached their zenith following the 1969 U.S. Supreme Court case *Tinker v. Des Moines*,[1] have been in steady decline since the mid-1980s. In addition, First Amendment rights for students at public colleges and universities were becoming increasingly restricted as the twenty-first century began.

CENSORSHIP IN PUBLIC SECONDARY SCHOOLS

The Supreme Court, in *Tinker v. Des Moines*, was asked to consider for the first time whether a public school district was justified in suspending students who wore black armbands to demonstrate their opposition to the

Vietnam War. John Tinker, 15, his sister Mary Beth Tinker, 13, and a 16-year-old friend, Christopher Eckhardt, wore the armbands to school one day in 1965 despite an order by their principal banning such armbands. The Tinkers and Eckhardt appealed the school district's decision to U.S. district court, where they encountered a less-than-sympathetic U.S. district judge, Roy Stephenson. Stephenson ruled in 1966 that the school board was justified in prohibiting the students from wearing armbands to school, noting that students have First Amendment rights but stating that school officials have great latitude in maintaining discipline in the classroom.[2] Stephenson wrote that school officials had a responsibility to maintain "a scholarly, disciplined atmosphere" in the classroom and had not only the right but also the obligation to prevent disruptions: "A subject should never be excluded from the classroom merely because it is controversial. It is not unreasonable, however, to regulate the introduction and discussion of such subjects in the classroom. The avowed purpose of the plaintiffs in this instance was to express their views on a controversial subject by wearing black armbands in the schools. While the armbands themselves may not be disruptive, the reactions and comments from other students as a result of the armbands would be likely to disturb the disciplined atmosphere required for any classroom."[3] Stephenson wrote further that the Tinkers and Eckhardt were free to wear their armbands outside of school on their own time, hence their First Amendment rights suffered only minor harm. Stephenson's ruling was upheld by a split Eighth Circuit Court of Appeals in a brief per curium, or unsigned, order.[4] But the U.S. Supreme Court, in a 7–2 ruling, overturned the district court decision, declaring that the wearing of armbands was symbolic speech protected by the First Amendment.[5] As Justice Fortas wrote for the majority, "It can hardly be argued that either students or teachers shed their constitutional rights to freedom of speech or expression at the schoolhouse gate."[6] That portion of the Court's decision is often quoted as a clarion call for students' free expression rights. In its decision, however, the Court distinguished between protected student expression and expression that "would materially and substantially interfere with the requirements of appropriate discipline in the operation of the school."[7] The Court specifically rejected Stephenson's position that school administrators have wide latitude in determining what expression would be disruptive and therefore could be prohibited. As the Court noted, "The District Court concluded that the action of the school authorities was reasonable because it was based upon their fear of a disturbance from the wearing of the armbands. But, in our system, undifferentiated fear or apprehension of disturbance is not enough to overcome the right to freedom of expression."[8]

For more than 15 years following *Tinker,* students won repeated victories in their battles for free expression rights. But that support for student expression began to shift, when a more liberal Supreme Court headed by Chief Justice Earl Warren shifted to a more conservative court headed by Chief Justice Warren Burger. In 1986, the Court was presented with a case that would allow it to step back from the *Tinker* decision, *Bethel School District v. Fraser.*[9] Matthew Fraser had been suspended from school for three days and barred from speaking at graduation after he made a nominating speech for a student government candidate at a school assembly. That nominating speech was filled with sexual innuendo, including statements that the "candidate is firm in his pants," is a "man who will take an issue and nail it to the wall," and who will "go to the very end—even the climax—for each and every one of you."[10] Lower courts ruled that Fraser's punishment violated First Amendment rights as the Supreme Court had articulated them in *Tinker*. But the Supreme Court upheld Fraser's punishment: "The freedom to advocate unpopular and controversial views in schools and classrooms must be balanced against the society's countervailing interest in teaching students the boundaries of socially appropriate behavior."[11] The Court recognized the value in protecting true political speech as was done in *Tinker*, especially when the views may be unpopular. But while the Court in *Tinker* ruled that expression was protected unless it materially and substantially disrupted the classroom, the Court in *Fraser* found a distinction between that type of protected expression and expression that is merely offensive: "Even the most heated political discourse in a democratic society requires consideration for the personal sensibilities of the other participants and audiences."[12] In doing so, the Court placed a greater premium on "the shared values of a civilized social order"[13] than on *Tinker's* protection of expression in schools.

Two years later, the Supreme Court stepped even further away from *Tinker* in the 1988 *Hazelwood v. Kuhlmeier*[14] case. The Supreme Court for the first time addressed the question of whether censorship of student expression in the school newspaper was unconstitutional. In the *Hazelwood* case, students enrolled in a Journalism II course at Hazelwood East High School in Missouri attempted to publish an edition of the school newspaper containing two stories that the principal disliked. One was based on interviews with students (identified with pseudonyms) who had become pregnant. The principal contended the students still could be identified by other details in the story. The second article discussed the impact of divorce on some students. The principal said the article was unfair because the divorced parents were not contacted to give their side of the story. The *Hazelwood* opinion, written by Justice White, found a difference between purely personal student expression, as in *Tinker*, and expression using a school name and resources, as in the high school newspaper. Similarly, the Court distinguished traditional public forums, such as sidewalks or street corners where anyone can assemble and express opinions, from a student newspaper published as part of the curriculum, in which the public does not have a reasonable expectation of access. In the case of student publications produced as part of the curriculum, the Court stated, educators can exercise editorial control over the "style and content" of school-sponsored student expression "as long as their actions are reasonably related to legitimate pedagogical concerns."[15] Among those pedagogical concerns, according to the *Hazelwood* decision, was "speech that is...ungrammatical, poorly written, inadequately researched, biased or prejudiced, vulgar or profane, or unsuitable for immature audiences."[16]

In both *Fraser* and *Hazelwood*, the Supreme Court ruled in a First Amendment case that, unlike the *Tinker* standard, school officials had wide latitude in determining what student expression to prohibit because of its content, even when that content did not disrupt school discipline. Under *Hazelwood*, school officials' ability to control student expression extends beyond the student press to all school-sponsored student expression, such as a play put on as part of a drama class or an afterschool club, a student-produced literary magazine published through an English class, or even a choral or band concert that is prepared by a music class. As the Court noted in its decision, a school must be able to take into account the

emotional maturity of the intended audience in determining whether to disseminate student speech on potentially sensitive topics, which might range from the existence of Santa Claus in an elementary school setting to the particulars of teenage sexual activity in a high school setting. A school must also retain the authority to refuse to sponsor student speech that might reasonably be perceived to advocate drug or alcohol use, (or) irresponsible sex.[17]

In the years following *Hazelwood*, a number of lower courts ruled in favor of administrators restricting student expression. In one case remarkably similar to the *Tinker* case, Alameda High School students in Colorado were barred from wearing blue and silver ribbons on their graduation gowns as a show of respect for the families of victims of the Columbine High School shootings, in which two gun- and bomb-wielding students had killed 12 other students and a teacher before turning the guns on themselves.[18] The students, aided by the American Civil Liberties Union, filed for an emergency temporary restraining order barring enforcement of the ban. Unlike the Supreme Court in 1969, however, U.S. District Judge Walker D. Miller ruled Alameda High School seniors could not wear the ribbons on the gowns, thereby upholding a Jefferson County school system policy that forbids adornment on graduation gowns, based on a concern that allowing one type of ornamentation might open the door to other types the community might find offensive. In this statement, Miller bypassed the precedent in *Tinker* that mere potential for disruption is not grounds for stifling student expression. During a hearing on the students' appeal of the school board policy, Miller stated that limitation of the First Amendment right to freedom of expression is permitted "so long as it is narrowly tailored to serve the governmental interests." Since public schools are funded by the local, state, and federal governments, Miller was making the connection that any expression that hampers school administrators' attempts to run their schools could be prohibited, no matter whether that expression is political speech as protected by *Tinker*.

Another method of restricting student expression has been to punish students for what they say or do outside of class. This has been a particularly troubling area for the courts when students, on their own time and using their personal computers, write and post derogatory comments about their schools or school officials on the Internet. In the early twenty-first century, a number of schools around the country, including schools in Indiana, Washington State, and New York City, adopted policies regulating student use of Web-based programs such as My Space and Facebook, even outside of class. The Clark-Pleasant School District in Indiana, for instance, enacted a blogging policy in October 2006 that prohibited students from accessing social networks such as My Space from school as well as posting harmful or threatening content outside of school. A New York City Department of Education policy that went into effect in the 2006–2007 school year included punishments ranging from suspension to expulsion for students posting "a threat of violence, injury or harm" on and off campus.[19]

Some judges, however, have ruled that penalizing students for what they produce at home goes too far, but the record is far from clear. In a 1998 Missouri case, a U.S. district judge overturned a student's punishment for a Web page he produced at home on his own time.[20] A federal court in Seattle ruled in 2000 that a school could not suspend a student who created mock obituaries for his classmates on a Web site he created on his home computer.[21] A U.S. district judge in Pennsylvania ruled in 2001 that a school could not punish a student for an e-mail he posted from his home computer ridiculing the school's athletic director.[22] A year later, the Pennsylvania Supreme Court ruled the opposite way, saying a student could be disciplined for a personal Web site that made a threat against a teacher, because other students accessed the site at school.[23]

In 2007, the U.S. Supreme Court issued a ruling concerning student expression that may have major ramifications for future court cases. A student at a Juneau, Alaska, high school was among students dismissed from class so that they could watch the Winter Olympics torch being carried past their school by runners. During the event, Joseph Morse held up a sign, which he described as nonsensical, which read, "Bong Hits 4 Jesus." School officials suspended Morse for advocating drug use during a school event, and he appealed. The Supreme Court upheld his suspension in *Morse v. Frederick,* stating that the event was a school event and that schools are within their authority to punish students for advocating drug use.[24]

In the wake of school shootings, such as the one in 1999 at Columbine High School in Colorado, school authorities throughout the nation reacted with renewed restrictions on student expression, usually citing the need to maintain safety. In the weeks following the Columbine shootings, for instance, school officials in Pennsylvania strip-searched a 14-year-old girl and suspended her for two weeks because she commented, during a classroom discussion about the Colorado shootings, that she could understand how unpopular students could be pushed so far that they would lash out violently. A South Carolina student was suspended for four days because his Web site said members of his ROTC unit "can eat feces and die." A nine-year-old boy in Maryland was given an in-school suspension for waving a drawing of a gun in his classroom. A student at Noronia Hills High School in Ohio was suspended and threatened with criminal charges for publishing a satirical horoscope in the student newspaper urging students to relieve stress by "blowing up your house, and then moving on to bigger stress-relieving activities, such as assassinating the president or wearing hats to school." School officials also confiscated copies of the newspaper after they were distributed.[25]

PUBLIC COLLEGES AND UNIVERSITIES

It has been well established that students at privately operated campuses are not entitled to all the First Amendment rights that are afforded their public school counterparts. An attempt to circumvent that exemption for private schools was attempted but failed in a 1971 lawsuit in U.S. district court in New York. In *Post v. Payton,*[26] the former director at WCWP-FM at Long Island University, some members of the radio station's student staff, and listeners challenged the university's decision to suspend operation of the station because of the airing of obscenities. The plaintiffs argued that because the school had obtained a Federal Communications Commission (FCC) license for the FM station, the privately financed school was effectively converted into an agent of government action, and as such the station was subject to First and Fourteenth Amendment protections. The district judge ruled against the claim, stating that mere federal licensing of a radio station is not enough to convert an otherwise-private institution into a government agency.

Any doubts that the *Tinker* standard granting students First Amendment rights applied to public higher education students were eliminated in 1972 in *Healy v. James*,[27] when the Court made it clear, while overturning Central Connecticut State College's refusal to recognize the radical leftist Students for a Democratic Society as an authorized campus association, that "state colleges and universities are not enclaves immune from the sweep of the First Amendment."[28]

Public college and university administrators have tried to control the content of student-run newspapers through a variety of means in the years since *Tinker* and *Healy*, and until 2006 virtually all those methods were ruled by the courts to be an abridgment of First Amendment rights. In one such method, campus administrators have attempted to punish editors, either through firing, suspension, or outright expulsion, for printing "improper" or "indecent" material. In *Trujillo v. Love*,[29] the managing editor of the Southern Colorado State University student newspaper, *The Arrow*, was suspended from her job for attempting to publish an editorial cartoon criticizing the university president and for submitting to the paper's faculty adviser a proposed editorial criticizing a municipal judge. In ordering Dorothy Trujillo reinstated as managing editor, the district court held that she had been improperly punished for exercising her right of free expression. The issue of punishing students for printing or attempting to print unpopular commentary reached the U.S. Supreme Court two years later in *Papish v. Board of Curators of the University of Missouri, et al.*, when a graduate student at the University of Missouri was expelled for distributing on campus an underground newspaper that school officials said contained "indecent speech."[30] In ordering the student's reinstatement, the Court said it was clear her expulsion was caused by the content of the newspaper, and not permissible rules regulating the time, place, and manner of its distribution, stating, "We think *Healy* makes it clear that the mere dissemination of ideas—no matter how offensive to good taste—on a state university campus may not be shut off in the name alone of 'conventions of decency.' "[31]

The courts have long held that college and university administrators are not permitted to reduce or eliminate funding for campus newspapers as an expression of discontent with the paper's content. In *Joyner v. Whiting*,[32] for instance, the Fourth Circuit Court of Appeals rejected an attempt by the president of North Carolina Central University to stop publication of the campus newspaper, *The Campus Echo*, by revoking all university funding and refunding all student fees used to finance the paper. The university president did so because he disagreed with the editorial stands taken by the newspaper's editors. But as the appeals court wrote in its decision reinstating funding of *The Echo*: "It may well be that a college need not establish a campus newspaper, or, if a paper has been established, the college may permanently discontinue publication for reasons wholly unrelated to the First Amendment.

But if a college has a student newspaper, its publication cannot be suppressed because college officials dislike its editorial comment."[33]

Likewise, in *Stanley v. McGrath*,[34] the Eighth Circuit Court of Appeals struck down a University of Minnesota Board of Regents policy that permitted students at the Twin Cities campus to obtain refunds of the portion of their mandatory student fees used to finance the *Minnesota Daily*, the campus newspaper. The board of regents took this action because of objections to a 1979 "Finals Week" edition of the paper that satirized Christ, the Roman Catholic Church, public figures, ethnic groups, and others. The appeals court found that the refund system at the University of Minnesota was based on administrators' objections to the paper's content and was therefore a violation of the First Amendment: "A public university may not constitutionally take adverse action against a student newspaper, such as withdrawing or reducing the paper's funding, because it disapproves of the content of the paper."[35]

Whereas these cases involved overall funding of the student newspaper, *Antonelli v. Hammond* showed that administrators cannot limit student newspapers by a one-time restriction of funding, either.[36] In *Antonelli*, the district court ruled that the Fitchburg State College president violated students' First Amendment protections when he refused funding for an issue of the campus newspaper, *The Cycle*, that he felt was obscene. The Court ruled that by refusing funding for the issue, the college president was restricting the flow of information to solely that approved of by an agent of the state government.

A third method of administrative control over student publication, perhaps more common, is through official university censors. In *Antonelli*, in addition to prohibiting the college president from cutting funding for the student-run newspaper, the district court barred university officials from requiring that future issues of the publication be approved by an advisory board appointed by the school president. However, a decision in the Seventh Circuit Court of Appeals,[37] a ruling that the Supreme Court refused to reconsider and therefore let stand, poses the possibility that the *Hazelwood* standard of allowing administrative censorship of student expression could be expanded to include higher education. The case, *Hosty v. Carter*, dealt with a Governors State University administrator's decision to require that the student newspaper be reviewed by her office before it could be printed; she told the private printing company that had been contracted to print the paper that it would not be paid if it printed the paper without her authorization.[38] The Seventh Circuit Court of Appeals held in 2005 that college administrators do have some control over the content of print media, and the Supreme Court in 2006 refused to review that ruling.

The consequence of that *Hosty* ruling, if it eventually is applied beyond the three states of the Seventh Circuit, is that the rights to freedom of expression that college and university students have enjoyed since the early 1970s could be lost to the more restrictive standards set out for secondary school students in *Hazelwood.*

SPEECH CODES

What about administrative limits on expression that are necessary to ensure that all students have access to a quality education without fearing reprisals from bigots? In response to increasingly common reports of intolerant, offensive speech and conduct on campus, more than 200 colleges and universities instituted "speech code" policies during the 1980s aimed at disciplining students for public displays of intolerance.[39] These codes varied in their approach, but most authorized official university punishment for violators who engaged in racist, sexist, or other hate speech aimed at individuals or groups and intended to convey a negative assessment of the targets because of their membership in a historically oppressed group.[40] Some codes were restricted to personal attacks, whereas others were broad enough to include the written word or even editorial cartoons published in a campus newspaper.[41]

There can be no doubt that hate speech is hurtful and aims to degrade the target in the crudest of manners. It can cause humiliation, shock, outrage, and even physical pain when aimed at individuals.[42] All members of the vilified group can suffer emotionally and physically.[43] Proponents of campus speech codes have also pressed the argument that hate speech, in addition to inflicting emotional pain, causes all members of the denigrated group to suffer a loss in the community, preventing them from full participation in educational opportunities.[44] As Robert M. O'Neill, former president of both the University of Virginia and the University of Wisconsin, writes, "Anyone who believes that speech codes reflect an artificial or imaginary condition are either ignorant or naïve."[45]

Campus officials' ability to limit expression through speech codes, however, suffered a setback with a pair of court rulings striking down codes at two midwestern universities as unconstitutional. The first of these decisions came in *Doe v. University of Michigan,*[46] in which the University of Michigan's speech code was overturned. The code had established a three-tiered system of tolerable and intolerable speech and conduct, with behavior that "stigmatizes or victimizes an individual on the basis or race, ethnicity, religion, sex, sexual orientation, national origin, ancestry, age, marital status, handicap or Vietnam-era veteran status" outlawed in most academic locations.[47] The District Court for the Eastern District of Michigan struck down the policy as unconstitutionally overbroad, applying to conduct permitted under the First Amendment. Relying on *West Virginia State Board of Education v. Barnette,*[48] in which the Supreme Court barred the public schools from forcing adherents of the Jehovah's Witness sect to participate in the Pledge of Allegiance, the Michigan court quoted the oft-cited statement, "If there is any star fixed in our constitutional constellation, it is that no official, high or petty, can prescribe what shall be orthodox in politics, nationalism, religion, or other matters of opinion or force citizens to confess by word or act their faith therein."[49] In this vein, the court noted that under the Constitution, no expression can be prohibited merely because it offends some people.[50] By prohibiting expression that "stigmatizes or victimizes" individuals, the Court said, the University of Michigan had violated the well-established constitutional protection of unpopular speech. In addition, the court noted, "These principles acquire a special significance in the university setting, where the free and unfettered interplay of competing views is essential to the institution's educational mission."[51]

Two years after *Doe,* the district court in Wisconsin visited the same territory. In *UWM Post v. Board of Regents of U. of Wisconsin,*[52] a speech code in the University of Wisconsin system was challenged by several plaintiffs, including the student newspaper at the University of Wisconsin at Milwaukee, as an infringement of First Amendment free speech rights.[53] The University of Wisconsin–Milwaukee code, enacted after a series of racially insensitive incidents on campus, prohibited expression that demeaned the sex, religion, color, creed, disability, sexual orientation, national origin, ancestry, or age of an individual or individuals and created an "intimidating, hostile or demeaning environment" for education or university-related work.[54] As in *Doe,* the court in *UWM Post* found that the speech code was impermissible censorship of free expression. The court noted that the university system's board of regents had a compelling interest in increasing diversity on its campuses. "However," the court stated, "the UW Rule does as much to hurt diversity as it does to help it. By establishing content-based restrictions on speech, the rule limits the diversity of ideas among students and thereby prevents the 'robust exchange of ideas' which intellectually diverse campuses provide."[55]

Both the *Doe* and *UWM Post* courts agreed that the only permissible content-based restriction on hate speech must follow the rule set down in *Chaplinsky v. New Hampshire,*[56] in which the Supreme Court permitted restriction of "fighting words"—"those which by their very utterance...intend to incite an immediate breach of the peace."[57] As the court in *UWM Post* stated, "The problems of bigotry and discrimination sought to be addressed here are real and truly corrosive of the educational environment. But freedom of speech is almost absolute in our land and the only restrictions the fighting words doctrine can abide is that based on the fear of violent reaction. Content-based prohibitions such as that in the UW Rule, however well intentioned, simply cannot survive the screening that our Constitution demands."[58]

In a third case indirectly involving speech codes, the Supreme Court in 1992 struck down a municipal hate speech code in *R.A.V. v. City of St. Paul.*[59] The ordinance at the heart of the case made it a misdemeanor to display any symbol or other object, including a Nazi swastika or a burning cross, that "one knows or has reasonable grounds to know arouses anger, alarm or resentment in others on the basis of race, color, creed, religion or gender."[60] In its decision, the Court found that any content-based regulation of expression is presumptively invalid under the First Amendment and that an ordinance that goes beyond the fighting words doctrine to limit unpopular expression, as the St. Paul ordinance did, is unconstitutional. "The point of the First Amendment is that the majority preferences must be expressed in some fashion other than silencing speech on the basis of its content."[61]

As a result of these court rulings, administrators at a number of universities tried a different approach in the 1990s and early 2000s, placing restrictions not on *what* was said but on *where* it was said. "Free speech zones" were created on campus where students and nonstudents could state their opinions, such as a pavilion, gazebo, or small outdoor stage. When free speech advocates challenged these speech zones as unconstitutional, many campuses altered or abandoned their policies. One such example occurred at what was then Southwest Missouri State University (now Missouri State University), where the board of governors approved a request from administrators to allow free speech only in an area about 40 feet square outside the campus bookstore, the "Bear Paw" area. University officials defended their decision by saying they did not want students on their way to or from class to be harassed by speakers with whom they might not agree. When challenged in U.S. district court by a student, however, the university changed its policy to allow free speech anywhere on campus except in classroom buildings during the hours classes are in session and in dormitory hallways. Similar speech zone policies at other state-supported schools also underwent changes at campuses across the country.

In contrast, speech codes that prohibit fighting words pass constitutional muster and are permitted. These codes prohibit personal attacks on individuals that meet the standard set out by the Supreme Court in the 1942 case *Chaplinsky v. New Hampshire.*[62] That case dealt with a man who stood on a street corner (the very definition of a free speech area, called a "public forum") and called a city marshal a series of vile names. The Court ruled that fighting words, that is, words that by their very utterance might incite the object of those words to retaliate with his or her fists, are not protected by the First Amendment as free speech. Campus speech codes that prohibit fighting words meet the requirements of the First Amendment and do not violate students' constitutional rights.

CONCLUSION

Does the principal at a public junior high school or high school have the right or the responsibility to ensure that student expression is acceptable? What about a college administrator? On one hand, school administrators on both levels believe that they have the responsibility to maintain a learning atmosphere. If that means placing limits on student expression, so be it. On the other, students attempting to express opinions that may conflict with those administrators' goals may be striving toward what the Supreme Court has called in numerous decisions the "marketplace of ideas," where a variety of viewpoints are given an airing, with the audience picking the best ideas.

Lower-court cases demonstrate the impact that the *Fraser* and *Hazelwood* decisions can have on student expression. In *Poling v. Murphy,* the Sixth U.S. Circuit Court of Appeals ruled in 1989 that a Tennessee student's criticism of school administrators was punishable under *Hazelwood,* including barring him from running for student body president.[63] A district judge in Idaho, citing *Fraser,* ruled that a public school was justified in the two-day suspension of a student who created and sold T-shirts depicting three school administrators as drunk.[64]

Justice Mary Muehlen Maring of the North Dakota Supreme Court, in a speech presented at Concordia College in March 1998 and reprinted in the *North Dakota Law Review,* agreed that students' free expression rights have been in steady decline since the mid-1980s, noting that in decisions such as *Fraser* and *Hazelwood* the Supreme Court has stepped away, at least in student First Amendment cases, from the doctrine that regulating student expression because of its content is prohibited: "Seemingly, once student expression falls outside the category of political speech, school administrators are given broad authority to look away from the effect of the student expression and instead to regulate based on the content of the expression."[65]

Primary and secondary school officials are more willing, following *Hazelwood,* to restrict expression that is socially unacceptable, criticizes administrators, or deviates from the mainstream. Their college counterparts may be willing to do the same thing on their campuses in the wake of the *Hosty* decision. A more conservative judicial system seems more willing to expand the categories of unprotected student expression, and therefore appeals of student expression restrictions are having limited success.

NOTES

1. *Tinker v. Des Moines Independent School District,* 393 U.S. 503 (1969).

2. *Tinker v. Des Moines Independent School District,* 258 F. Supp. 971 (S. D. Iowa 1966).

3. Ibid. at 953.

4. *Tinker v. Des Moines Independent School District,* 383 F.2d 988 (8th Cir. 1967).

5. *Tinker,* 393 U.S.

6. Ibid. at 506.

7. Ibid. at 513.

8. Ibid. at 508.

9. *Bethel School District v. Fraser,* 478 U.S. 675 (1986).

10. Ibid. at 687.

11. Ibid.

12. Ibid.

13. Ibid. at 683.

14. 484 U.S. 260 (1988).

15. Ibid. at 581.

16. Ibid.

17. Ibid. at 272.

18. Charlie Brennan and John Ingold, "Judge Bans 'CHS' on Graduation Gowns," *Denver Rocky Mountain News,* May 22, 1999.

19. April Hale, "Probing Policies: High Schools Enacting Policies to Punish Students for Social Networking Sites Created outside School," *SPLC Report* 28, no. 1 (Winter 2006–2007): 6.

20. *Beussnik v. Woodland R-IV School Dist.,* No. I:98CV00093 (E.D. Mo. 1998).

21. "Off Campus, Not Off Limits: School Responses to Online Bullying Is the New Threat to Off-Campus Speech," *SPLC Report* 25, no. 1 (Winter 2003–2004): 33.

22. "Federal Court Rules School District Violated Rights of High School Student Suspended for E-Mail," *SPLC Newsflash,* March 29, 2001 (accessed November 29, 2007, at www.splc.org/newsflash.asp?id=256&year=2001).

23. Ibid.

24. *Morse v. Frederick,* 127 S. Ct. 2618 (2007).

25. Mark Paxton, "Student Free Expression Rights and the Columbine Shootings," *Free Speech Yearbook* 37 (1999): 135–43.

26. 323 F. Supp. 799 (1971).

27. 408 U.S. 169 (1972).

28. Ibid. at 180.

29. 322 F. Supp. 1266 (1971).

30. 410 U.S. 667 (1973).

31. Ibid. at 670.

32. 477 F.2d 456 (1973).

33. Ibid. at 460.

34. 719 F.2d 279 (1983).

35. Ibid. at 582.

36. 308 F. Supp. 1329 (1970).

37. The states that comprise the Seventh Circuit are Illinois, Indiana, and Wisconsin.

38. 412 F.3d 731 (2005).

39. "Campus Speech Codes," *CQ Researcher* 18 (January 8, 1993): 18.

40. William A. Kaplin, "A Proposed Process for Managing the First Amendment Aspects of Campus Hate Speech," *Journal of Higher Education* 62 (1992): 518.

41. Ibid.

42. Ibid.

43. Ibid., 519.

44. Ibid. See, generally, Mari Matsuda, "Public Response to Racist Speech: Considering the Victim's Story," *Michigan Law Review* 87 (1989): 2320.

45. Robert M. O'Neill, *Free Speech in the College Community* (Bloomington: Indiana University Press, 1997), 2.

46. 721 F. Supp. 852 (E.D. Mich. 1989).

47. Ibid. at 856. Publications sponsored by the university, such as the student newspaper, were expressly not subject to regulation under the policy.

48. 319 U.S. 624 (1943).

49. Ibid. at 642.

50. *Doe,* 721 F. Supp. at 863.

51. Ibid.

52. 774 F. Supp. 1163 (E.D. Wis. 1991).

53. Kate Culver, "The Campus v. the Workplace: University Hate Speech Codes and Hostile Environment Law" (paper presented at Association for Education in Journalism and Mass Communication Annual Meeting, Kansas City, August 10–14, 1993).

54. *UWM Post,* 774 F. Supp. at 1165.

55. Ibid. at 1176.

56. 315 U.S. 568 (1942).

57. Ibid. at 571–72.

58. *UWM Post,* 774 F. Supp. at 1181.

59. 112 S. Ct. 2538 (1992).

60. Ibid. at 2541.

61. Ibid. at 2548.

62. 315 U.S.

63. 872 F.2d 757 (6th Cir. 1989).

64. *Gano v. School District,* 674 F. Supp. 796 (1987).

65. Mary Muehlen Maring, "'Children Should Be Seen and Not Heard': Do Children Shed Their Right to Free Speech at the Schoolhouse Gate?" *North Dakota Law Review* 74 (1998): 679–89.

7

The Future of Censorship

Where does censorship go from here? How do technological developments interact with the government's attempts to limit access to "harmful" material? If the past is any guide, the development of technology is accompanied by both a fear of the technology and a desire to limit the effect of that technology.

Perhaps the best example of this phenomenon was the development of the printing press and the British government's attempt to require licensing and prior approval of any printed matter. Not only did the printing press make mass production of printed matter possible, it also created a demand for literacy. A reading, thinking public was a threat to the Crown. Of course, attempts to limit the content of and access to printed material were doomed to failure, and one of the outcomes was our own Constitution and the First Amendment guaranteeing freedom of the press.

Samuel Morse's development of the telegraph enabled long-distance delivery of messages, and the U.S. government attempted to limit delivery of material over the telegraph during the Civil War to prevent distribution of information useful to the enemy. The development of radio led to the creation of a federal bureaucracy in the form of the Federal Radio Commission, later the Federal Communications Commission (FCC), to regulate stations and their content. When television came along, this same federal bureaucracy regulated it as well.

The Internet prompted fears that inappropriate content would be made available to young people, prompting Congress to pass the Communication Decency Act (CDA), later ruled unconstitutional; the Children's Internet

Protection Act, requiring libraries to have filters on publicly accessible computers; and the Child Online Protection Act, which as of this writing appears to be headed for the same fate as the CDA because lower courts have ruled it unconstitutional and the Supreme Court has raised questions about it, although without actually ruling on its merits.

There is no question that the Internet is home to inappropriate material; a quick perusal of the World Wide Web on any computer not equipped with a filter will uncover plenty of sites that obviously violate obscenity law. The problem in enforcing obscenity law on the Internet is twofold. First, state obscenity laws are virtually impossible to enforce because the Internet has no boundaries, so that state officials are often unable to apply their state laws. Second, it is often difficult, if not impossible, to track down who is responsible for the vast array of sexually explicit material on the Web. Material is posted, reposted, and reposted again.

As with the Internet, if history has taught us anything, it is that new methods of delivering information will continue to be developed, and with those new delivery methods, someone will attempt to censor them.

Take reading books, for instance. Several companies are developing portable handheld devices that will allow readers to download the latest book to be read on screen at the reader's convenience wherever the reader wants to read.[1] Considering this country's long history of banning and even burning books, how will the government react to the prospect of sending books over the airwaves to handheld devices? Will the FCC, as part of its 1934 mandate to regulate communication via radio and wire, have carte blanche to regulate these e-books? What will happen when children have access to these devices? Will Congress step in with a new version of the Communication Decency Act to bar harmful electronic books from impressionable young readers? No one ever won election to any public office on a platform of making adult-oriented books available to children, and the history of congressional attempts to place restrictions on the Internet makes it likely some legislator will attempt to place similar restrictions on the availability of electronic books to children, ignoring the court record that such attempts at regulating the Internet have been ruled to be violations of the First Amendment.

Another question concerns the ways these electronic books will revolutionize the library field, for both public and school libraries. One of the vexing issues facing school libraries has been the selection of books. As the Supreme Court noted in the *Pico* case, school officials have wide latitude in selecting which books will be added to the shelves of public school libraries, but once the books are on the shelves, the officials have less ability to remove the books because of parents' complaints. If books are available online, will the library selection process change? In public libraries, the federal government already requires filters on publicly accessible computers; the question is to what extent this filtering requirement might be extended to electronic books. The principal issue is the same: underage library patrons having access to material that the federal government considers to be inappropriate for them.

Then there are the ubiquitous cell phones, with their instant messaging capabilities and their ability to take still photos and video, all of which can be sent point-to-point. Already, everyday consumers armed with cell phone cameras have revolutionized the news-gathering field; virtually anything that anyone does in public, or even in private, is now a potential photo or video that might appear on You-Tube, TMZ, or some other Web site. Do these picture-taking, cell phone–using people violate the public's right to privacy? The FCC already regulates the cell phone industry in terms of what frequencies they can use and what customer policies they must follow. The FCC also prohibits broadcasters from airing indecent programming under the *Pacifica* ruling. It does not take a tremendous leap of the imagination to conceive of a situation in which the FCC decides to regulate the transmission of images over cell phone networks.

Meanwhile, the FCC has been giving conflicting signals about regulating over-the-air broadcasting. On the one hand, as illustrated by the campaign against indecency that prompted record-setting fines against radio shock jock Howard Stern and against CBS for the ill-fated Janet Jackson Super Bowl halftime show, the FCC is extremely hands-on for the broadcasters it regulates. On the other hand, the FCC has been moving for years toward increased deregulation of the economic side of broadcasting; at the end of 2007, for example, the FCC reversed decades of precedent and voted to allow cross-ownership of newspapers and television stations in the nation's 20 largest markets, ignoring complaints that allowing one company to own both a paper and a television station will reduce the diversity of news and other programming available to consumers.[2] In a previous decision to further deregulate the television industry, the FCC had voted to increase the maximum number of stations one company could own nationwide, but it was overruled by Congress. Under pressure from Congress, which, in the wake of the Janet Jackson episode, considered legislation to increase the maximum fine for broadcasters that air indecency, the FCC seems unlikely to take any action loosening the reins on the decency standards for the nation's radio and television stations.

In addition, the FCC has started to impose some of the same restrictions on satellite television as on over-the-air broadcasting, for example, that satellite delivery systems that generate their own advertising have to abide by the requirements that broadcasters provide reasonable access to the airwaves for candidates for president, vice president, U.S. representative, and U.S. senator—the federal elected officials—in the 45 days before a primary election and 60 days before a general election, plus providing equal opportunity to all candidates for an office once one candidate is given or sold airtime.[3] It is not a great leap to consider that other FCC regulations, including the ban on indecency, could be imposed not only on satellite TV but also the growing field of satellite radio.[4]

Over-the-air television (now more often delivered by cable or satellite) has been pushing the boundaries of decency since the 1970s, and this continued pushing of the envelope means that the FCC will continue to monitor—and fine—stations that violate indecency standards. Traditional over-the-air radio also faces increased FCC scrutiny as shock jocks continue to offend.

The Federal Election Commission (FEC), meanwhile, attempted in 2004 to impose restrictions on bloggers who post their personal dispatches on the Internet if the comments concerned candidates for election, making such blogging subject to FEC reporting requirements just as anyone who spends money to influence an election must file financial reports; after a public outcry and news media ridicule, the FEC stepped back from its proposed rules. The question remains: are bloggers journalists? Are they protected by state shield laws, which generally protect journalists in those states from being forced to disclose their sources? Or are they something different—personal observers who give their opinions without worrying about original reporting? The debate over the role of bloggers will occupy journalists and their critics for a long time to come.

Other areas of performing and visual arts will continue to draw government objections, especially when they use federal funding such as National Endowment for the Arts grants. Senator Jesse Helms may be gone from the scene, but there is no shortage of members of Congress who will campaign on the platform of enforcing decency standards in the arts. Plays that push the edge with nudity or language will continue to face objections from local officials, and there will certainly be renewed attempts in Congress to impose restrictions on the performing arts.

The time of censorship of movies, however, appears to have passed with the end of the Hays Code and the Legion of Decency. Mainstream movies are still subject to ratings, but movie producers who refuse to abide by the MPAA's ratings code can still distribute their movies, perhaps because of the huge economic force that the movie industry wields.[5]

Censorship of music seems destined to continue. Jazz was criticized when it replaced classical music as the choice for young people, rock was censored when it replaced jazz, and rap has been censored as it replaces rock. It seems certain that the next development in popular music will likewise face opposition. The proliferation of personal music listening devices, such as iPods and MP3 players, means that new music can spread more rapidly than in the days when radio stations determined what music people listened to. The widespread distribution of that new music, whatever it is, might mean it is spread much faster and farther than previous new musical genres.

One method of spreading music, however, already ran into a roadblock in the courts, which have ruled that computer software designed to allow peer-to-peer music sharing over the Internet, such as Napster[6] or Grokster,[7] violates the rights of those who produced the music being shared and therefore violates federal copyright law.

Restriction on student expression appears to be one area of law where censorship is clearly increasing. Because of 1988's *Hazelwood* decision, public school students face restrictions on what they write at school or on their computers from home and even what signs they hold as they stand on the streets. For college students, the *Hosty* decision, while technically applying only to the states in the Seventh Circuit Court of Appeals—Illinois, Indiana, and Wisconsin—opens the door for universities in other states to impose censorship on student expression.[8]

The program of embedding journalists with military units during times of war, despite critics who complained that it isolated reporters and made them less likely to write negative stories, appears to be a trend that will continue when the United States next goes to war. As stated earlier in this chapter, however, cell phone technology makes it possible for anyone to be a photojournalist.

Finally, censorship of dissent, which has been around in America since the Federalists and the Republicans and the Sedition Act of 1798, shows no sign of ending. The USA PATRIOT Act has the potential to criminalize the advocating of opinions that differ from the official position of the federal government. It allows federal investigators to subpoena and review individual patrons' library records, as well as permitting warrantless interception of phone calls, without notice to the people whose material is being reviewed.

The First Amendment, ratified as part of the Bill of Rights in 1791, has vexed America for more than 200 years. What did the founding fathers mean when they wrote that "Congress shall make no law respecting an establishment of religion or prohibiting the free exercise thereof; abridging freedom of speech or of the press; or the right of the people peaceably to assemble, and to petition the Government for a redress of grievances"? Does "no law" mean no law? Or, as has been the case throughout American history, does "no law" mean that restrictions are acceptable for speech or press that expresses dissent, occurs during wartime, expresses graphic sexuality, is made by students, or meets any of the dozens of other instances in which the First Amendment did not protect speech or the press?

Because of the spread of media, from print and broadcasting, to the Internet and personal communication devices (such as cell phones and

Blackberry-type personal digital assistants), many Americans believe that censorship died with the dawning of the twentieth century and affects no one in the twenty-first century. Those same people may wonder why a book about censorship even needs to be written. Based on the material in this book, it is clear that America does indeed have a rich tradition of censorship and restriction on expression. It is also clear that censorship, which some people see as a relic of the past, has never ended and will continue as we move through the twenty-first century.

NOTES

1. Steven Levy, "The Future of Reading," *Newsweek,* November 26, 2007, 54. Amazon is one of the primary developers of this technology.

2. Frank Aherns, "Divided FCC Enacts Rules on Media Ownership," *Washington Post,* December 19, 2007.

3. Public Interest Obligations, 47 CFR Sec. 25.701.

4. Peter Lauria, "Satellite Pleads by Citing Diversity," *New York Post,* March 22, 2007, 42. Some members of Congress have already started seeking legislation to make satellite radio subject to FCC jurisdiction.

5. Moviegoers spent $9.7 billion at the box office in 2007. See Brooks Barnes, "A Film Year Full of Escapism, Flat in Attendance," *New York Times,* January 2, 2008 (accessed January 7, 2008, at www.nytimes.com/2008/01/02/movies/02year.html). This does not take into account the billions of dollars spent on DVDs each year.

6. *A & M Records, Inc. v. Napster,* 239 F.3d 1004 (9th Cir. 2001).

7. *Metro-Goldwyn-Mayer Studios Inc v. Grokster,* 545 U.S. 913 (2005).

8. See the Student Press Law Center Web site at www.splc.org to keep up-to-date on developments involving student expression rights.

Timeline of Censorship in the United States

1735	John Peter Zenger is acquitted of seditious libel. He was charged because of criticism he published about New York's colonial governor, William Cosby.
1791	The First Amendment, guaranteeing freedom of speech and the press, is ratified as part of the Bill of Rights.
1798	The Sedition Act is enacted, making it a federal crime to criticize the president, members of Congress, or the government.
1815	Jesse Sharpless becomes the first person in the United States convicted of obscenity.
1861	Censorship of news reporting during wartime is imposed during the Civil War for the first time.
1873	Congress passes the Comstock Act, making it a crime to send indecent material through the mail. Antipornography crusader Anthony Comstock is placed in charged of enforcing the law.
1915	Supreme Court rules that movies are not protected by the First Amendment.
1917	Federal government imposes voluntary censorship on newspapers and strict censorship on war correspondents as the United States enters World War I.
1917–1918	The Espionage Act and Sedition Act make it a federal crime to speak against the war effort or impede the draft. These acts are upheld in a series of Supreme Court decisions, including one, *Schenck,* in which Justice Oliver Wendell Holmes states that the

government can prohibit speech that presents a "clear and present danger," such as falsely shouting "Fire!" in a theater.

1919 Socialist and former presidential candidate Eugene Debs is convicted of violating the Espionage Act.

1919 Justice Oliver Wendell Holmes argues in a dissent in the *Abrams* case that the best test of speech is not prohibition but the free marketplace of ideas.

1925 The Supreme Court, in the *Gitlow* case, uses the 14th Amendment to make the First Amendment apply to state government.

1931 The Supreme Court, in *Near v. Minnesota,* for the first time strikes down a state law restricting expression, ruling that prior restraint on the press is the exception and not the rule.

1934 Movies begin to be reviewed by the Hays Code, created by the motion picture industry, and the Catholic Church's Legion of Decency.

1934 Congress creates the Federal Communications Commission (FCC) to regulate radio and, later, television and other electronic media.

1930s The Federal Bureau of Investigation (FBI), under Director J. Edgar Hoover, begins surveillance of suspected dissidents.

1940 Congress passes the Smith Act, making it a crime to be a member of the Communist Party or advocate overthrow of the government.

1940s Strict censorship on war correspondents is imposed during World War II, and newspapers engage in voluntary self-censorship in the United States.

1942 Supreme Court upholds New Hampshire law forbidding "fighting words" in *Chaplinsky* case.

1951 The Supreme Court upholds the Smith Act in the *Dennis* case. It was later ruled to be a violation of the First Amendment in *Yates* in 1957.

1952 Supreme Court, reversing its 1915 decision, rules that movies are protected by the First Amendment.

1957 Supreme Court rules in *Roth* that First Amendment does not protect obscenity and attempts to define obscenity. Court also says a work has to be judged in its entirety in determining whether it is obscene.

1967 Troops use force to prevent an antiwar rally in Washington, D.C.

1969 Supreme Court rules in the *Tinker* case that public school students retain First Amendment rights in school, as long as they do not create a material disruption of the classroom.

1960s–'70s	Reporters in Vietnam are free to report war with no censorship.
1960s–'70s	Federal government, FBI, Central Intelligence Agency (CIA), and army engage in widespread spying and disruption of antiwar groups.
1971	Supreme Court rules in Pentagon Papers case that the federal government could not prohibit the *New York Times* and *Washington Post* from publishing articles based on stolen classified documents detailing U.S. involvement in the Vietnam War.
1973	Supreme Court outlines a three-part definition of obscenity in *Miller.*
1975	Supreme Court rules that theater productions are protected by the First Amendment.
1982	Supreme Court rules in *Pico* case that once school administrators put a book in a school library, they cannot remove it because of complaints about the content.
1983	News media are blocked from reporting war in Grenada, the first time reporters were not allowed to cover troops in combat.
1985	Congress, spurred by the Parents Music Resource Center, holds hearings on proposals to require parental warnings on music recordings.
1988	Supreme Court rules in *Hazelwood* case that school officials can censor high school publications produced as part of the curriculum.
1989	Supreme Court in *Texas v. Johnson* rules that a federal law banning burning of the U.S. flag is in violation of the First Amendment.
1990	Congress passes law restricting National Endowment for the Arts funding for indecent art.
1997	Supreme Court in *Reno v. ACLU* overturns the Communication Decency Act, which attempted to make the Internet off-limits to anything indecent or inappropriate for minors to view.
1998	Congress reacts to the *Reno* decision by enacting the Child Online Protection Act, requiring age verification for sexually explicit Web sites.
2002	Pentagon allows embedded reporters during Iraq War, with journalists assigned to specific military units.

Bibliography

COURT CASES AND OTHER LEGAL MATERIAL

A & M Records, Inc. v. Napster, 239 F.3d 1004 (9th Cir. 2001).

AAMA v. Kendrick, 244 F.3d 572 (7th Cir. 2001).

Abrams v. U.S., 249 U.S. 631 (1919).

American Booksellers v. Hudnut, 771 F.2d 323 (7th Cir. 1985).

Antonelli v. Hammond, 308 F. Supp. 1329 (D.C. Mass. 1970).

Ashcroft v. ACLU, 542 U.S. 656 (2004).

Bethel School District v. Fraser, 478 U.S. 675 (1986).

Beussnik v. Woodland R-IV School Dist., 30 F. Supp. 2d 1175 (E.D. Mo. 1998).

Boorda v. Subversive Activities Control Board, 421 F.2d 1142 (D.C. Cir. 1969).

Brandenburg v. Ohio, 343 U.S. 444 (1969).

Burstyn v. Wilson, 343 U.S. 495 (1952).

Campbell v. St. Tammany Parish School Board, 64 F.3d 184 (5th Cir. 1995).

Chaplinsky v. New Hampshire, 315 U.S. 568 (1942).

Child Online Protection Act, 47 U.S.C. § 231, 1998.

Cohen v. California, 403 U.S. 15 (1971).

Commonwealth of Massachusetts v. Holmes, 17 Mass. 336 (Mass. Sup. Ct. 1821).

Commonwealth of Pennsylvania v. Sharpless, 2 Serg. & R. 91 (Pa. Sup. Ct. 1815).

Counts v. Cedarville School District, 295 F. Supp 2d 996 (W.D. Ark. 2003).

Debs v. U.S., 249 U.S. 211 (1919).

Dennis v. U.S., 341 U.S. 494 (1951).

Doe v. University of Michigan, 721 F. Supp. 852 (E.D. Mich. 1989).

ESA v. Granholm, 426 F. Supp. 2d 646 (E.D. Mich. 2006).

FCC v. Pacifica, 438 U.S. 726 (1978).

Fleischfresser v. Directors of School District 200, 15 F.3d 680 (7th Cir. 1994).

Gano v. School District, 674 F. Supp. 796 (D.C. Idaho 1987).

Gilbert v. Minnesota, 254 U.S. 325 (1920).

Ginsberg v. N.Y., 390 U.S. 629 (1968).

Ginzburg v. U.S., 383 U.S. 463 (1966).

Gitlow v. New York, 268 U.S. 652 (1925).

Griswold v. Connecticut, 381 U.S. 479 (1958).

Grove Press v. Christenberry, 175 F. Supp. 488 (S.D. N.Y. 1959).

Grove v. Mead School District No. 354, 753 F.2d 1528 (9th Cir. 1985).

Halsey v. the New York Society for the Suppression of Vice, 136 N.E. 219 (N.Y. Ct. App. 1922).

Hazelwood v. Kuhlmeier, 484 U.S. 260 (1988).

Healy v. James, 408 U.S. 169 (1972).

Hosty v. Carter, 412 F.3d 731 (7th Cir. 2005).

In re Worthington, 30 N.Y.S. 361 (1894).

In the Matter of Violent Television Programming and Its Impact on Children, FCC 07–50, 22 FCCR 7929, MB 04–261, April 25, 2007.

ISDA v. St. Louis County, Mo., 329 F.3d 954 (8th Cir. 2003).

Island Trees Union Free School District v. Pico, 457 U.S. 853 (1982).

Jacobellis v. Ohio, 378 U.S. 184 (1964).

Joyner v. Whiting, 477 F. 2d 456 (4th Cir. 1973).

Kingsley International Pictures v. the Regents of the University of the State of New York, 360 U.S. 684 (1959).

Korematsu v. U.S., 323 U.S. 214 (1944).

Luke Records v. Navarro, 960 F.2d 134 (11th Cir. 1990).

Manual Enterprises v. Day, 370 U.S. 478 (1962).

Masses Publishing Co. v. Patten, 244 F. 536 (S.D. N.Y. 1917).

Memoirs v. Massachusetts, 383 U.S. 413 (1966).

Metro-Goldwyn-Mayer Studios Inc v. Grokster, 545 U.S. 913 (2005).

Miller v. California, 413 U.S. 15 (1973).

Mishkin v. N.Y., 383 U.S. 502 (1996).

Morse v. Frederick, 127 S. Ct. 2618 (2007).

Mozert v. Hawkins County Board of Education, 827 F.2d 1058 (6th Cir. 1987).

Mutual Film Co. v. Hodges, 236 U.S. 248 (1915).

Mutual Film Corp. v. Industrial Commission of Ohio, 236 U.S. 230 (1915).

NEA v. Finley, 524 U.S. 569 (1992).

Near v. Minnesota, 283 U.S. 697 (1931).

New York Times v. U.S., 403 U.S. 713 (1971).

New York v. Ferber, 458 U.S. 474 (1983).

Osborne v. Ohio, 495 U.S. 103 (1990).

Papish v. Board of Curators of the University of Missouri, et al., 410 U.S. 667 (1973).

Paris Adult Theatre I v. Slaton, 413 U.S. 49 (1973).

Poling v. Murphy, 872 F.2d 757 (6th Cir. 1989).

Pope v. Illinois, 481 U.S. 497 (1987).

Post v. Payton, 323 F. Supp. 799 (E.D. N.Y. 1971).

Public Interest Obligations, 47 CFR Sec. 25.701.

R.A.V. v. City of St. Paul, 112 S. Ct. 2538 (1992).

Red Lion Broadcasting v. FCC, 395 U.S. 367 (1969).

Reno v. ACLU, 521 U.S. 844 (1997).

Renton v. Playtime Theater, 479 U.S. 41 (1986).

Roth v. U.S., 354 U.S. 476. (1957).

Schenck v. U.S., 249 U.S. 47 (1919).

Skywalker Records v. Navarro, 739 F. Supp. 578 (S.D. Fla. 1990).

Smith v. California, 361 U.S. 147 (1959).

Southeastern Promotions Ltd. v. Conrad, 420 U.S. 546 (1975).

Spence v. Washington, 418 U.S. 405 (1974).

Stanley v. Georgia, 394 U.S. 557 (1869).

Stanley v. McGrath, 719 F.2d 279 (8th Cir. 1983).

Street v. New York, 394 U.S. 576 (1974).

Texas v. Johnson, 497 U.S. 3897 (1989).

Tinker v. Des Moines Independent School District, 258 F. Supp. 971 (S. D. Iowa 1966).

Tinker v. Des Moines Independent School District, 383 F.2d 988 (8th Cir. 1967).

Tinker v. Des Moines Independent School District, 393 U.S. 503 (1969).

Trujillo v. Love, 322 F. Supp. 1266 (D. Colo. 1971).

United Artists Corporation et al. v. Board of Censors of City of Memphis et al., 189 Tenn. 397 Tenn. Sup. Ct. 1949).

United States v. Kennerly, 209 F. 119 (S.D. N.Y. 1913).

United States v. One Book Called "Ulysses," 5 F. Supp. 182 (S.D. N.Y. 1933).

United States v. One Book Called "Ulysses," 72 F.2d 705 (2nd Cir. 1934).

U.S. v. Britton, 17 Fed. 131 (1883).

U.S. v. Eichman, 496 U.S. 310 (1990).

U.S. v. Paramount Pictures, 334 U.S. 131 (1948).

U.S. v. Playboy Entertainment Group, 589 U.S. 803 (2000).

UWM Post v. Board of Regents of U. of Wisconsin, 774 F. Supp. 1163 (E.D. Wis. 1991).

Video Software Dealers Ass'n v. Schwarzenegger, 401 F. Supp. 2d 1034 (N.D. Cal. 2005).

Virgil v. School Board of Columbia County, 677 F. Supp. 1547 (M.D. FL 1988).

Virgil v. School Board of Columbia County, 862 F.2d 1517 (11th Cir. 1988).

West Virginia State Board of Education v. Barnette, 319 U.S. 624 (1943).

Winters v. New York, 333 U.S. 507 (1948).

Writers Guild of America W., Inc. v. FCC, 423 F. Supp. 1064, 1161 (C.D. Calif. 1976).

Yates v. U.S., 354 U.S. 298 (1957).

Young v. American Mini Theaters, 427 U.S. 50 (1976).

WEB SITES

www.aclu.org. The American Civil Liberties Union, for information about civil liberties issues and cases.

www.afa.org. The American Family Association, a clearinghouse for issues on expression.

www.eagleforum.org. The Eagle Forum Education and Legal Defense Fund, for a conservative perspective on education, media, and other issues.

www.freedomforum.org. The Freedom Forum, for information about First Amendment issues and news.

www.splc.org. The Student Press Law Center, for information and news about student expression rights.

BOOKS AND BOOK CHAPTERS

Alvino, James. "Is It Book Burning Time Again?" in *Censorship and Education,* edited by Eli M. Oboler, 32. New York: H. H. Wilson, 1981.

Andrew, Christopher. *For the President's Eyes Only: Secret Intelligence and the American Presidency from Washington to Bush.* New York: HarperCollins, 1995.

Aronson, James. *The Press and the Cold War.* New York: Bobbs Merrill, 1970.

Austin, Aleine. *Matthew Lyon: "New Man" of the Democratic Revolution, 1749–1822.* University Park: Pennsylvania State University Press, 1981.

Baran, Stanley J., and Dennis K. Davis. *Mass Communication Theory: Foundations, Ferment and Future.* Belmont, CA: Wadsworth, 2000.

Becker, Beverly C., and Susan M. Stan. *Hit List for Children 2: Frequently Challenged Books.* Chicago: American Library Association, 2002.

Bezner, Lili Corbus. *Photography and Politics in America: From the New Deal into the Cold War.* Baltimore: Johns Hopkins University Press, 1999.

Black, Gregory D. *The Catholic Crusade Against the Movies: 1940–1975.* Cambridge, UK: Cambridge University Press, 1997.

Black, Gregory D. *Hollywood Censored: Morality Codes, Catholics and the Movies.* Cambridge: Cambridge University Press, 1994.

Bosmajian, Haig A. *Obscenity and Freedom of Expression.* New York: Burt Franklin, 1976.

Brancato, Robin F. "In Defense of: *Are You There God? It's Me, Margaret, Deenie,* and *Blubber*—Three Novels by Judy Blume." In *Censored Books—Critical Viewpoints,* edited by Nicholas Karolides, Lee Buress, and John M. Kean, 87–97. Lanham, MD: Scarecrow Press, 1993.

Broun, Heywod, and Margaret Leech. *Anthony Comstock, Roundsman of the Lord.* New York: Literary Guild of America, 1927.

Buress, Lee, Nicholas J. Karolides, and John M. Kean. "Introduction." In *Censored Books: Critical Viewpoints,* edited by Nicholas Karolides, Lee Buress, and John M. Kean, xii–xiv. Lanham, MD: Scarecrow Press, 1993.

Candor-Chander, C. A. "A History of the Kanawha County Textbook Controversy, April 1974–April 1975." EdD diss., Virginia Polytechnic Institute and State University 1976.

Capps, Walter H. *The New Religious Right: Piety, Patriotism, and Politics.* Columbia: University of South Carolina Press, 1990.

Carmilly-Weinberger, Moshe. *Fear of Art: Censorship and Freedom of Expression in Art.* New York: R. R. Bowker, 1986.

"Christian Coalition Presents Contract with the American Family." In *The New Christian Right: Political and Social Issues,* edited by Melvin I. Urofsky and Martha May, 198. New York: Garland, 1996.

Chunovic, Louis. *One Foot on the Floor: The Curious Evolution of Sex on Television from* I Love Lucy *to* South Park. New York: TV Books, 2000.

Clapp, Jane. *Art Censorship: A Chronology of Proscribed and Prescribed Art.* Metuchen, NJ: Scarecrow Press, 1972.

Cowan, Geoffrey. *See No Evil: The Backstage Battle over Sex and Violence on Television.* New York: Simon and Schuster, 1979.

Cronkite, Walter. *A Reporter's Life.* New York: Alfred A. Knopf, 1996.

Cumings, Bruce. *War and Television.* London: Verso, 1992.

Dadge, David, *Casualty of War: The Bush Administration's Assault on a Free Press.* Amherst: Prometheus Books, 2004.

Desmond, Robert W. *Tides of War: World News Reporting 1940–1945.* Iowa City: University of Iowa Press, 1984.

Diamond, Sara. *Not by Politics Alone: The Enduring Influence of the Christian Right.* New York: Guilford Press, 1998.

Dickerson, Donna Lee. *The Course of Tolerance: Freedom of the Press in Nineteenth Century America.* New York: Greenwood Press, 1990.

Doyle, Robert. *Banned Books: 2000 Resource Guide.* Chicago: American Library Association, 2000.

Dubin, Steven C. *Arresting Images: Impolitic Art and Uncivil Actions.* New York: Routledge, 1992.

Eaton, Clement. *The Freedom-of-Thought Struggle in the Old South.* New York: Harper Torchbooks, 1964.

Emery, Edwin. *The Press and America: An Interpretive History of the Mass Media.* Englewood Cliffs, NJ: Prentice-Hall, 1972.

Ewing, Joseph H. "The New Sherman Letters." In *Newsmen and National Defense: Is Conflict Inevitable?* edited by Lloyd J. Matthews, 19–29. Washington: Brassley's, 1991.

Final Report of the Attorney General's Commission on Pornography. Nashville, TN: Rutledge Hill Press, 1986.

Fraleigh, Douglas M., and Joseph S. Tuman. *Freedom of Speech in the Marketplace of Ideas.* New York: St. Martin's Press, 1997.

Frohnmayer, John. *Out of Tune: Listening to the First Amendment.* Nashville, TN: The Freedom Forum First Amendment Center, 1994.

Gaddy, Barbara B., T. William Hall, and Robert J. Marzano. *School Wars: Resolving Our Conflicts over Religion and Values.* San Francisco: Jossey-Bass, 1996.

Gardner, Gerald. *The Censorship Papers: Movie Censorship Letters from the Hays Office, 1934 to 1968.* New York: Dodd, Mead & Co., 1987.

Gilmore, Mikal. *Night Beat: A Shadow History of Rock and Roll.* New York: Doubleday, 1998.

Gore, Tipper. "Rock Music Should Be Labeled." In *Culture Wars: Opposing Viewpoints,* edited by Fred Whitehead, 185–193. San Diego: Greenhaven Press, 1984.

Hallin, Daniel C. *The 'Uncensored War': The Media and Vietnam.* New York: Oxford University Press, 1986.

Hammond, William M. "The Army and Public Affairs: A Glance Back." In *Newsmen and National Defense: Is Conflict Inevitable?* edited by Lloyd J. Matthews, 1–16. Washington: Brassley's, 1991.

Haney, Robert W. *Comstockery in America: Patterns of Censorship and Control.* Boston: Beacon Hill Press, 1960.

Harris, Brayton. *Blue and Gray in Black and White: Newspapers in the Civil War.* Washington, DC: Bratsford Brassey, 1999.

Hefley, James. *Are Textbooks Harming Your Children? Norman and Mel Galber Take Action and Show You How!* Milford, MI: Mott Media, 1979.

Heins, Marjorie. *Sex, Sin and Blasphemy: A Guide to America's Censorship Wars.* New York: New Press, 1993.

Helms, Jesse. *Here's Where I Stand.* New York: Random House, 2005.

Hentoff, Nat. *The First Freedom: The Tumultuous History of Free Speech in America.* New York: Delacorte Press, 1980.

Hentoff, Nat. *Free Speech for Me But Not for Thee: How the American Left and Right Relentlessly Censor Each Other.* New York: HarperPerennial, 1992.

Hoffman, Fred S. "The Panama Press Pool Deployment: A Critique." In *Newsmen and National Defense: Is Conflict Inevitable?* edited by Lloyd J. Matthews, 91–109. Washington: Brassley's, 1991.

Hirsch, Tim. "Banned by Neglect: *Tom Sawyer,* Teaching the Conflicts." In *Censored Books II: Critical Viewpoints, 1985–2000,* edited by Nicholas Karolides, 1–9. Lanham, MD: Scarecrow Press, 2002.

Hirschon, Stanley P. *The White Tecumseh: A Biography of William T. Sherman.* New York: John Wiley and Sons, 1997.

Hoskins, Andrew. Televising War from Vietnam to Iraq. London: Continuum, 2004.

Houchin, John. *Censorship of the American Theatre in the Twentieth Century.* Cambridge: Cambridge University Press, 2003.

Kammen, Michael. *Visual Shock: A History of Art Controversies in American Culture.* New York: Alfred A. Knopf, 2006.

Karolides, Nicholas J., Margaret Bald, and Dawn B. Sova. *100 Banned Books: Censorship Histories of World Literature.* New York: Checkmark Books, 1999.

Kilpatrick, James Jackson. *The Smut Peddlers.* Westport, CT: Greenwood Press, 1960.

Kristol, Irving. "Pornography, Obscenity and the Case for Censorship." In *The Neocon Reader,* edited by Irwin Stelzer, 169–180. New York: Grove Press, 2004.

Lande, Nathaniel. *Dispatches from the Front: News Accounts of American Wars, 1776–1991.* New York: Henry Holt, 1995.

Laufe, Abe. *The Wicked Stage: A History of Theater Censorship and Harassment in the United States.* New York: Frederick Ungar, 1978.

Levy, Leonard W. *Freedom of the Press from Zenger to Jefferson.* New York: Bobbs-Merrill, 1966.

Lewis, Anthony. *Make No Law: The Sullivan Case and the First Amendment.* New York: Vintage Books, 1993.

Lynes, Russell. *The Tastemakers.* New York: Harper and Brothers, 1954.

Massie, Dorothy. "Censorship in the Schools." In *Censorship and Education,* edited by Eli M. Oboler, 78. New York: H. H. Wilson, 1981.

Matthews, Lloyd J. "Preface." In *Newsmen and National Defense: Is Conflict Inevitable?* edited by Lloyd J. Matthews, ix–xii. Washington: Brassley's, 1991.

Miller, Arthur. "On Censorship." In *Censored Books: Critical Viewpoints,* edited by Nicholas Karolides, Lee Buress, and John M. Kean, 4. Lanham, MD: Scarecrow Press, 1993.

Mitchell, W.J.T. "The Violence of Public Art: Do the Right Thing." In *Art and the Public Sphere,* edited by W.J.T. Mitchell, 29–47. Chicago: University of Chicago Press, 1992.

Mock, James R. *Censorship 1917.* Princeton, NJ: Princeton University Press, 1941.

Noble, William. *Bookbanning in America: Who Bans Books and Why.* Middlebury, VT: Paul S. Eriksson, 1990.

Noebel, David A. *The Marxist Minstrels: A Handbook of Communist Subversion of Music.* Tulsa, OK: American Christian College Press, 1974.

O'Neill, Robert M. *Free Speech in the College Community.* Bloomington: Indiana University Press, 1997.

Oboler, Eli M. "Introduction." In *Censorship and Education,* edited by Eli M. Oboler, 9–10. New York: Wilson, 1981.

Orman, John. *The Politics of Rock Music.* Chicago: Nelson-Hall, 1984.

Patrick, J. Max. *The Prose of John Milton.* New York: New York University Press, 1968.

Paul, Christopher, and James J. Kim. *Reporters on the Battlefield: The Embedded Press in Historical Context.* Arlington, VA: Rand Corporation, 2004.

Putnam, William Lowell. *John Peter Zenger and the Fundamental Freedom.* Jefferson, NC: McFarland, 1997.

Ravitch, Diane. *The Language Police: How Pressure Groups Restrict What Students Learn.* New York: Alfred A. Knopf, 2003.

Reynolds, Donald E. *Editors Make War: Southern Newspapers in the Secession Crisis.* Nashville, TN: Vanderbilt University Press, 1970.

Robbins, Louise S. *Censorship and the American Library: The American Library Association's Response to Threats to Intellectual Freedom, 1939–1969.* Westport, CT: Greenwood Press, 1996.

Rubin, Maria, Jacqueline Livingston, Marilyn Zimmerman, and Betsy Schneider. "'Not a Pretty Picture': Four Photographers Tell Their Personal Stories about Child 'Pornography' and Censorship." In *Censoring Culture: Contemporary Threats to Free Expression,* edited by Robert Atkins and Svetlana Mintcheva, 213–227. New York: New Press, 2006.

Sharkey, Jacqueline. *Under Fire: U.S. Military Restrictions on the Media from Grenada to the Persian Gulf.* Washington, DC: Center for Public Integrity, 1991.

Siegel, Paul. *Cases in Communication Law.* Boston: Allyn and Bacon, 2002.

Skinner, James M. *The Cross and the Cinema: The Legion of Decency and the National Catholic Office for Motion Pictures, 1933–1970.* Westport, CT: Praeger, 1993.

Smith, Jeffrey A. *War and Press Freedom: The Problem of Prerogative Power.* New York: Oxford University Press, 1999.

Souli, Sofia A. *Love Life of the Ancient Greeks.* Athens, Greece: Toubis, 1997.

Sova, Dawn B. *Banned Plays: Censorship History of 125 Stage Dramas.* New York: Facts on File, 2004.

Stolz, Mary. "White-Outs and Black-Outs on the Book Shelves." In *Censored Books: Critical Viewpoints,* edited by Nicholas Karolides, Lee Buress, and John M. Kean, 36. Lanham, MD: Scarecrow Press, 1993.

Stone, Geoffrey. *Perilous Times: From the Sedition Act of the 1790s to the War on Terrorism.* New York: W. W. Norton, 2004.

Stone, Geoffrey R. *War and Liberty. An American Dilemma: 1790 to the Present.* New York: W. W. Norton, 2007.

Sweeney, Michael S. *Secrets of Victory: The Office of Censorship and the American Press and Radio in World War II.* Chapel Hill: University of North Carolina Press, 2001.

Weaver, Russell L., Andrew T. Kenyon, David F. Partlett, and Clive P. Walton. *The Right to Speak Ill: Defamation, Reputation and Free Speech.* Durham, NC: Carolina Academic Press, 2006.

Wertham, Fredric. *Seduction of the Innocent.* Toronto: Clarke, Irwin & Co., 1954.

Willey, Barry E. "Military-Media Relations Come of Age." In *Newsmen and National Defense: Is Conflict Inevitable?* edited by Lloyd J. Matthews, 81–89. Washington: Brassley's, 1991.

Woodward, Gary C. "The Rules of the Game: The Military and the Press in the Persian Gulf War." In *The Media and the Persian Gulf War,* edited by Robert E. Denton Jr., 1–26. Westport, CT: Praeger, 1993.

ARTICLES

Aherns, Frank. "Divided FCC Enacts Rules on Media Ownership." *Washington Post,* December 19, 2007.

Barnes, Brooks. "A Film Year Full of Escapism, Flat in Attendance." *New York Times,* January 2, 2008. Accessed January 7, 2008, at www.nytimes.com/2008/01/02/movies/02year.html.

Blanchard, Margaret A., and John E. Semonche. "Anthony Comstock and His Adversaries: The Mixed Legacy of This Battle for Free Speech." *Communication Law and Policy* 11, no. 3 (2006): 317–66.

Braestrup, Peter. "Censored." *New Republic* 204, no. 6 (1991): 16–17.

Brennan, Charlie, and John Ingold. "Judge Bans 'CHS' on Graduation Gowns." *Denver Rocky Mountain News,* May 22, 1999.

Burton, Joseph. "Sidebar 3—Censorship of Comic Books Challenged by Defense Fund." *Serials Review* 20, no. 4 (1994): 58.

"Campus Speech Codes." *CQ Researcher* 18 (January 8, 1993): 18.

Cazan, Deborah. "Concerts: Rated or Raided?: First Amendment Implications of Concert-Rating." *Vanderbilt Journal of Entertainment and Law* 2 (Spring 2000): 170–83.

Cerf, Bennett. "War and Book Business." *Publishers Weekly,* March 28, 1942, 1248.

Cornehls, Jim. "The USA PATRIOT Act: The Assault on Civil Liberties." *Z Magazine,* July 2003, 35.

Culver, Kate. "The Campus v. the Workplace: University Hate Speech Codes and Hostile Environment Law." Paper presented at Association for Education in Journalism and Mass Communication Annual Meeting, Kansas City, August 10–14, 1993.

Davison, W. Phillips. "The Third-Person Effect in Communication." *Public Opinion Quarterly* 47 (1983): 1–15.

Eggen, Dan. "Ashcroft Defends Anti-Terrorism Steps: Civil Liberties Groups' Attacks 'Only Aid Terrorists,' Senate Panel Told." *Washington Post,* December 7, 2001.

Farley, Melissa. "Sex for Sale: Prostitution, Trafficking, and Cultural Amnesia: What We Must Not Know to Keep the Business of Sexual Exploitation Running Smoothly." *Yale Journal of Law and Feminism* 18 (2006): 109–44.

FCC Drops Fine over Eminem Song." Associated Press, January 9, 2002. Accessed November 3, 2007, at www.freedomforum.org.

"Federal Court Rules School District Violated Rights of High School Student Suspended for E-Mail." *SPLC Newsflash,* March 29, 2001. Accessed November 29, 2007, at www.splc.org/newsflash.asp?id=256&year=2001.

Fox, Mark A. "Market Power in Music Retailing: The Case of Wal-Mart." *Popular Music and Society* 28, no. 4 (2005): 507–19.

Galli, Mark. "Infection in the Body." *Christianity Today* 45, no. 4 (2001): 8.

Gladin, Susan. "Watching Out for Civil Liberties." *Chapel Hill Herald,* September 14, 2003, 2.

Hale, April. "Probing Policies: High Schools Enacting Policies to Punish Students for Social Networking Sites Created outside School." *SPLC Report* 28, no. 1 (Winter 2006–2007): 6.

Harrington, Richard. "The Capitol Hill Rock War; Emotions Run High as Musicians Confront Parents' Group at Hearing." *Washington Post,* September 20, 1985.

Hay, C. "Sex, Guns and Videotape: Music-Video Outlets Clean Up the Acts, Establishing Stricter Guidelines about What Can Be Aired." *Billboard,* December 1999, 40.

Henson, Robert. "The Muzzling of World War II Radio Weathercasts." *Weatherwise* 56, no. 3 (May–June 2003): 20–21.

Hightower, Jim. "Bush Zones Go National." *The Nation,* August 16/23, 2004, 29.

Hillocks, G. H., Jr. "Books and Bombs: Ideological Conflict and the Schools—A Case Study of the Kanawha County Book Protest." *School Review* 86 (August 1978): 632–54.

Hocklander, Sony. "Professor Leaves Evangel University after 'Full Monty' Role." *Springfield News-Leader,* September 26, 2006.

Huebner, Andrew J. "Rethinking American Press Coverage of the Vietnam War, 1965–68." *Journalism History* 31, no. 3 (2005): 150–61.

Hughes, John. "Pornography: The Social Ill behind Some Dangerous Crimes." *Christian Science Monitor,* August 16, 2006, 9.

Huston, Kristen. "'Silent Censorship': The School Library and the Insidious Book Selection Censor." *UMKC Law Review* 72 (Fall 2004): 241–55.

Ingles, Ian. "The *Ed Sullivan Show* and the (Censored) Sounds of the Sixties." *Journal of Popular Culture* 39, no. 4 (2006): 558–74.

"Kanawha PTA Board Opposes Certain Texts." *The Charleston Gazette,* June 19, 1974.

Kaplin, William A. "A Proposed Process for Managing the First Amendment Aspects of Campus Hate Speech." *Journal of Higher Education* 62 (1992): 518.

Kelley, Michael. "Banned in Memphis: City Has High Profile in Obscenity Case." *The Commercial Appeal,* June 1, 1995.

Lauria, Peter. "Satellite Pleads by Citing Diversity." *The New York Post,* March 22, 2007, 42.

Levy, Steven. "The Future of Reading." *Newsweek,* November 26, 2007, 54.

Lichtblau, Eric. "Gonzales Lays Out His Priorities at Justice Dept." *New York Times,* March 1, 2005.

MacKinnon, Catherine. "Pornography as Defamation and Discrimination." *Boston University Law Review* 71 (1991): 793–815.

Malone, Julia. "Antipornography Group Turns Senate Ear to Lurid Rock Lyrics." *Christian Science Monitor,* September 23, 1985, 24.

"Mapplethorpe Controversy Reverberates in Cincinnati 10 Years Later." The Associated Press, April 11, 2000, accessed November 2, 2007, at www.freedomforum. org.

Maring, Mary Muehlen. "'Children Should Be Seen and Not Heard': Do Children Shed Their Right to Free Speech at the Schoolhouse Gate?" *North Dakota Law Review* 74 (1998): 679–89.

Martin, James J. "Other Days, Other Ways: American Book Censorship 1918–1945." *Journal of Historical Review* 10, no. 2 (Spring 1990): 133–41.

Matsuda, Mari. "Public Response to Racist Speech: Considering the Victim's Story." *Michigan Law Review* 87 (1989): 2320.

Michael, Kay. "90,000 Textbooks Voted for Schools." *The Charleston Gazette,* November 9, 1974.

"Minister 'Praying God Will Strike Dead.'" *Sunday Gazette-Mail,* September 29, 1974.

Moen, Matthew. "The Preacher versus the Teacher." *NEA Higher Education Journal* 9, no. 1 (1993): 125–43.

"Off Campus, Not Off Limits: School Responses to Online Bullying Is the New Threat to Off-Campus Speech." *SPLC Report* 25, no. 1 (Winter 2003–2004): 33.

Page, A. L., and D. A. Clelland. "The Kanawha County Textbook Controversy: A Study of the Politics of Life Style Concern." *Social Forces* 57 (1978): 265–81.

Paulson, Kenneth. "Regulation through Intimidation: Congressional Hearings and Political Pressure on America's Entertainment Media." *Vanderbilt Journal of Entertainment and Law Practice* 7 (Winter 2004): 61–89.

Paxton, Mark. "Student Free Expression Rights and the Columbine Shootings." *Free Speech Yearbook* 37 (1999): 135–43.

Peltz, Richard J. "Pieces of *Pico:* Saving Intellectual Freedom in the Public School Library." *Brigham Young University Education and Law Journal* 2 (2005): 103–58.

Porch, Douglas. "'No Bad Stories': The American Media-Military Relationship." *Naval War College Review* 55, no. 1 (2002): 85–107.

Rather, Dan. "Truth on the Battlefield." *Harvard International Review* 23, no. 1 (Spring 2001): 66–71.

Robinson, Stephen. "Freedom, Censorship, Schools and Libraries." *English Journal* 70 (January 1981): 58–59.

Rothschild, Matthew. "Gagging Protesters by the Manual." *The Progressive,* September 2007, 16.

Schiovani, Yvonne, and Richard Haas. "Public Bus Drivers in Boycott." *Charleston Daily Mail,* September 10, 1974.

Schmetzer, Kate. "Fighting Porn." *Campus Life,* December 2005, 30.

"School Officials Waive Hearing." *Charleston Daily Mail,* November 23, 1974.

Stanton, Sam, and Emily Bazar. "Agents Abridge Rights." *The (Raleigh) News and Observer,* September 28, 2003.

Sumpter, Randall S. "'Censorship Liberally Administered': Press, U.S. Military Relations in the Spanish-American War." *Communication Law and Policy* 4, no. 4 (Autumn 1999): 463–81.

Sweeney, Michael S. "Censorship Missionaries of World War II." *Journalism History* 27 (2001): 4–13.

"U.S. Marshals to Enter Dispute." *The Charleston Gazette,* September 10, 1974.

Withrow, Lynn. "Splinter Text Group Hits Prominent Writers' Works." *Charleston Daily Mail,* November 1, 1974.

Index

About the Author

MARK PAXTON is a professor in the Department of Media, Journalism, and Film at Missouri State University, where he has taught since 1995. He has written extensively on First Amendment issues, particularly as they apply to college media and students' freedom of expression, and he has been active in the American Civil Liberties Union. Before entering academia, Paxton was a reporter and news editor for The Associated Press and for newspapers in West Virginia and Tennessee.